MW00814860

a Time to Grow

18 weeks to better
balance & boundaries
for busy women

Patricia R. Garey

PACIFIC PRESS® PUBLISHING ASSOCIATION
Nampa, Idaho
Oshawa, Ontario, Canada
www.PacificPress.com

Dedication

**This book is dedicated to my mothers, five extraordinary women
who have nurtured and inspired me with their love, their lives, and their faith:**

Elizabeth, my great-grandmother;
Ida and Myrtle, my grandmothers;
Toini, my spiritual mother;
&
my mother, Ida.

Copyright © 2003 by Pacific Press® Publishing Association.
Printed in United States of America.
All Rights Reserved.

Designed and illustrated by Michelle C. Petz

Additional copies of this book are available by calling toll free 1-800-765-6955 or visiting
http://www.adventistbookcenter.com.

Scripture references marked are from the New International Version. Copyright © 1973, 1978, 1984,
International Bible Society. Used by permission of Zondervan Bible Publishers.

Library of Congress Cataloging-in-Publication data:

Garey, Patricia R., 1956-
A time to grow : 18 weeks to better balance & boundaries for busy women / Patricia R. Garey.
p. cm.
ISBN: 0-8163-1961-8
1. Seventh-day Adventist women—Religious life. 2. Christian life—Seventh-day Adventist authors. I. Title.

BV4527.G37 2003
248.8'43'088267—dc21   2002045197

03 04 05 06 07 • 5 4 3 2 1

Introduction

Like many women of my generation, I have struggled to balance family, church, career, and relationship with God. But as both my family and my career expanded, I began to feel more and more as if I were rushing from one crisis to the next. The small consulting business begun in a corner of our bedroom grew to four offices with employees in several states. What started out as a stay-at-home job with flexible hours had turned into a demanding juggling act. Most days I felt that I had not served anybody well, least of all myself. In the wee hours of the morning, the discouragement and guilt would close in. My mind would race through lists and lists of things I should have done. I was convinced that if I could work just a little bit harder the next day, everything would be better. During those bouts of insomnia, it never occurred to me that I didn't need to learn how to work harder but how to enjoy life more.

One day while I was chatting with a psychologist friend of mine, she casually observed that as a group, "Adventist women seemed to have real boundary issues." I was immediately intrigued. "What do you mean we 'have real boundary issues'?" I asked. My friend explained that most of the clients she saw in the Loma Linda counseling center where she worked seemed to suffer from the same root problem. "They chronically neglect self-care in a mistaken belief that everyone else's needs are more important than their own. They suffer from an inability to set healthy boundaries." The inevitable results were depression, obesity, anxiety, and a host of other problems that followed, such as insomnia, addictions, co-dependency, and poor health.

I reluctantly recognized my increasing insomnia as a warning sign. I wondered if I, too, had boundary issues. I couldn't remember the last time I had exercised or read a book or spent some time alone. When would I find the time? Was taking care of myself really the last thing on my to-do list? It was obvious that I needed to make some changes before I totally compromised my health and emotional well-being. As I started to make self-care a priority, I was surprised to discover a wonderful resurgence of creative energy and, more important, joy. I have come to realize that striving for balance is a daily commitment.

In writing this book, I have attempted to encourage women to stop and smell the roses. *A Time to Grow* contains eighteen weeks of resources and spiritual meditations for busy women. *A Time to Grow* draws on "the garden season" as a metaphor and source of inspiration, although the personal journey outlined in *A Time to Grow* can be started anytime.

I have chosen to begin each week with a home or gardening idea. This book is not about homemaking or decorating, but I believe that once a week, no matter how busy we are, we should give ourselves permission to enjoy the simple pleasures of our home. Cultivating a garden is an incredibly healing and therapeutic activity. As we are learning to reestablish balance in our hectic lives, tending a garden slows us down and puts us back in touch with more natural rhythms.

Monday through Thursday I address a wide range of issues facing today's women. They include spiritual exercises, career strategy, family-and-friend activities, community-service ideas, personal- and creative-growth exercises, health issues, and relationship-building activities. Some exercises are challenging and will require you to focus on tough issues. Some will encourage you to take action or make choices. Some are playful and will ideally help you become more creative in your relationships. Each week I have also included a vegetarian recipe suggestion and a Sabbath afternoon activity to help busy moms with quick-and-easy ideas to make Sabbath a day to look forward to.

The daily Scripture reading is based on a simple formula to cover the entire Bible in a year by reading three chapters on weekdays and four chapters on Sabbath. The Bible readings alternate between the Old and New Testaments and have been selected to relate in a broad way to the topics.

God has certainly called women to many diverse tasks. He has called us to be wives and warriors, mothers and merchants, beauty queens and prophets. I pray that *A Time to Grow* will challenge you to embrace your personal calling and that God will bless you with the grace to live it well. It is my hope that *A Time to Grow* will be a small oasis on your journey, a place for you to nurture your soul, and a safe harbor to re-equip for the quest.

Particia R. Garey

Saturday Night Fever

It came as a surprise to me to discover that the infamous party of Simon the Pharisee, previously Simon the Leper, was a Saturday night party celebrating the Healer/Teacher, Jesus of Nazareth. For some reason, I had always pictured the events taking place on a lazy afternoon. Recasting those events into a Mediterranean evening at the close of the strictly observed Jewish Sabbath changes the entire story for me. I imagine Martha in a near fit of restrained frenzy, waiting for the last shadow to fall before flying into the kitchen. Early spring would mean that she had at least a couple of hours after sunset to serve up a fashionably late dinner. I imagine that the stuffed grape leaves had been prepared on Friday and were cooling on a tray in the well and that the firewood had been carefully stacked by the oven, ready to be tossed in the moment the last ray of sun disappeared from the courtyard. In all the hustle and bustle of the kitchen, Martha may have missed the drama of the evening as her sister crept out of the smoky shadows and threw herself upon the honored Guest in a very undignified display, drying the Man's feet with her hair, an action that undoubtedly brought Mary's previous profession to the front of everyone's mind. Even if it had been possible to politely ignore an emotional woman in the semi-darkness, the intense saturation of the night air with the expensive perfume would bring the party to a dead stop.

The silence is broken by a loud buzz of general disapproval. Mary sinks to the floor, realizing her mistake in using the perfume. She has publicly humiliated the One she loves. Christ sharply rebukes the judgmental crowd, Judas and Simon in particular. As Mary slinks off toward the kitchen in embarrassment, Judas backs into the shadows in disgust. He's putting in an appearance at another party before the evening is over. Christ has just insinuated that he, Judas, is a greedy liar! That was a mistake. He'll take thirty pieces of silver for that remark! His eyes glisten with hatred. Christ turns toward the shadows. Their eyes lock in the instant before Judas slips out the side door. Saturday night fever burns bright in Bethany—but the party is over.

THOUGHT TO PONDER

❧ If I picture myself at Simon's party, do I see myself as Martha, Mary, or part of the disapproving crowd?

> *"The glory of Christianity is to conquer by forgiveness."*
> —William Blake

AROMATIC GARDENS

We love gardens not only for the beautiful horticulture and soothing spaces but also for their wonderful aromas and fragrances. Every garden is improved with a few scented plants perfuming the breeze, even if the garden is only a window box. Following is a list of some well-known aromatic plants. Perhaps you remember a fragrance from your childhood or a special vacation. Why not indulge your sense of smell by planting a few aromatic plants this season?

Trees/Shrubs	Flowers/Herbs
Flowering fruit trees	Hyacinths
Pine trees	Lilies
Magnolia trees	Freesias
Lilac bushes	Roses
Cedar trees	Lavender
	Honeysuckle
	Gardenias
	Scented geranium
	Hyssop
	Sweet basil

The Scent of Sorrow

Scent is a powerful trigger. A familiar smell can send forgotten memories flooding back in brilliant detail, erasing time and distance in an instant, fragrant memories reminding us of people and places we have loved and lost. We close our eyes and inhale the essence of our memories, images so fragile, so fleeting, they evaporate into thin air as we exhale. Have you ever wondered how Mary Magdalene came to select a fragrance as her gift for Christ? It was such an expensive gift, a pint of pure nard. Why didn't she settle on something more substantial, something less fleeting? Wouldn't you have picked something that would have lasted longer? Or at least thought twice about pouring out the entire contents all at once?

I'm thinking I would have gone for a soft wool cloak woven from the finest Persian wool to keep my Lord warm and dry on His travels. Maybe a rare copy of the book of Isaiah on a scroll so that Christ could pour over it in the privacy of His own studies instead of having to go to the temple to read under the watchful eyes of the priests. An inlaid ivory walking stick from Ethiopia would support the Master as He traveled from town to town; someday perhaps it would become a scepter. I think I would have thought more along those lines if I were shopping for an extravagant gift in A.D. 32. How shortsighted and useless my gift would have been. Christ was crucified before the week was up. Mary had just a moment in time, and she poured out her love in one glorious, extravagant gesture. How did Mary come to select her gift for Christ? I've often wondered, haven't you?

THOUGHTS TO PONDER

❀ Did Mary understand that the things of the world were not the things Christ valued?

❀ If I had less than a week to express my love to a dear one, what would I give that person? Why not give that to him or her now?

"I tell you the truth, wherever the gospel is preached throughout the world, what she has done will also be told, in memory of her" (Mark 14:9).

THE BLACK SHEEP OF THE FAMILY

If you have a family like almost everybody else's, there are a few black sheep in the family fold. Sometimes our embarrassment over our loved ones' actions keeps them from returning to church. Even if they desire to revisit their spiritual roots, they are often keenly aware of how their appearance or habits will offend the other members of the congregation. Taking our cue from Christ, we might consider ways our church can welcome home black sheep and prodigal children. Do we have an open-door policy? How can we find ways to say with our words and our actions:

❀ You are welcome as you are—blue jeans, body art, jewelry, and extreme hair.
❀ You are welcome as you are—bad habits, smoky smells, and poor diet.
❀ You are welcome as you are—sad, depressed, divorced, or on parole.
❀ You are welcome as you are—doubting, unsure, tentative, even angry.
❀ You are welcome as you are—because Christ loves you and so do we!

Saints and Sinners

We think we know the difference, don't we? I've often heard it said, "I have pretty good instincts about people"—but I have never personally found that to be true. I am easily fooled. Based on the experience of more than a decade in the employment business, I think most people are easily fooled. Some people look so good on paper. Consider Simon's party for Jesus in Bethany a week before the Crucifixion. If you had been a member of that dinner party, would you have been able to discern the good from the bad? Simon's dinner party was attended by some of the most notorious saints and sinners who have ever lived. Would you have been able to pick them out? The twelve disciples were present, mostly laborers, fishermen, and farmers. They also included Matthew the tax collector, a corrupt government official, and Simon the Zealot, a former terrorist. Judas, on the other hand, had some abilities and polish. The host, Simon the Pharisee, according to some biblical scholars, had contributed to Mary's decent into prostitution. But as the host of this event, honoring a famous religious leader, he must have looked pretty good from the outside. Mary was trying to put her life back together, but she had suffered a whole string of setbacks and must have seemed a rather pitiable character. Martha and Lazarus, though, would appear to have been especially beloved by Christ.

Fast forward one week and one day to Sunday morning after the Crucifixion. The landscape has certainly changed, hasn't it? Whom is Christ waiting for in the garden before ascending to the Father? Not for Lazarus, so recently raised from the dead himself; not for Simon, His recent influential host. Not even for hardworking, loyal Martha. The Lord of the universe pauses before His triumphal ascension to the courts of glory to wipe away Mary's tears. By then, one of the party members has committed suicide. Would anyone have guessed that it would be Christ's self-assured business manager, Judas? And could we really have foreseen that the burly take-charge Peter would fold at a servant girl's taunt, bitterly denying Jesus? Saints or sinners—we really don't have a clue. Sometimes not even about ourselves. "There, but for the grace of God, go I."

THOUGHTS TO PONDER
❀ Am I ever overly impressed with the outward trappings of position and piety?
❀ Could I be more charitable in my regard for struggling new Christians?

"Man may dismiss compassion from his heart, but God never will."
—William Cowper, poet

PRAYER FOR A COMPASSIONATE HEART

The president of a successful research company once shared her morning routine with me. I found it deeply moving, an inspiring and uplifting way to start the day.

After completing her morning exercises, she would sit cross-legged on her exercise mat and close her eyes in prayer. She imagined her life as a series of concentric rings radiating outward. First, she would pray for God's blessing on herself, then for her children and her husband. Imagining her ever-widening circle of relationships, she would request God's blessing on her extended family, her friends, her coworkers. Before closing her prayer, she would implore God's blessing on her enemies and adversaries, those who had disappointed her, let her down, or desired to do her harm. She would remain in an attitude of prayer until God blessed her with a spirit of compassion and forgiveness for her enemies. Her last prayer was a prayer of thankfulness, and then she would rise to meet the day.

Midnight in the Garden of Good and Evil

In the 1994 bestseller *Midnight in the Garden of Good and Evil*, the reader soon discovers that nothing is quite as it seems. Investigating a murder in one of the oldest and most venerated neighborhoods of Savannah, Georgia, journalist John Berendt attempts to uncover the truth. On the surface, Savannah is a genteel and beautiful city, exquisitely designed with lush public gardens every few blocks. Behind the refined façades and hanging moss, however, is a completely different reality. Fraud, decadence, insanity, witchcraft, and criminal behavior of every ilk seethe just behind the pretty exteriors. On the cover of Berendt's book is a photograph of a statue of a beautiful young woman in the Bonaventure Cemetery in Savannah. The statue, of course, is a gravestone.

Christ used that symbolism long ago: "Woe to you . . . Pharisees, you hypocrites! You are like whitewashed tombs, which look beautiful on the outside but on the inside are full of dead men's bones and everything unclean" (Matthew 23:27).

That Saturday night as Judas made his way along the road to Jerusalem from Simon's party in Bethany, a few short miles away, Jerusalem must have looked beautiful. The crowds are beginning to drift in for the great religious festival, Passover. Their campfires flicker in the olive groves surrounding the city. Herod's temple glistens in the moonlight like a huge luminescent pearl. And at the very heart of that glorious edifice to Jehovah's glory, a clandestine party meets at midnight. Thirty pieces of silver exchange hands. A deal is struck.

THOUGHTS TO PONDER

❀ Appearances can be so deceiving. How can I teach my children discernment?

❀ Have I considered whether I am living an authentic life or a façade?

"The supreme end of education is expert discernment in all things—the power to tell the good from the bad, the genuine from the counterfeit, and to prefer the good and the genuine to the bad and the counterfeit."—Samuel Johnson

AUTHENTIC CHRISTIANITY

Hypocrisy is a common criticism of Christians. Christians will always experience a certain dissonance between the ideals we espouse and our day-to-day actions. The apostle Paul discussed the struggle in Romans 7. "I have the desire to do what is good, but I cannot carry it out" (Romans 7:18). However, erecting an elaborate façade does not solve the problem. We may not be perfect, but we can be honest and humble about our hopes as well as our failures. Take the following Hypocrisy Reality Check:

1. Are there areas of my life that I take great pains to hide from others?
2. Am I easily embarrassed by my children's or spouse's actions because I think it will reflect poorly on me?
3. Do I sometimes fib about my past or my accomplishments so people will think better of me?
4. Do I sometimes find myself publicly criticizing others to keep people from realizing that my life is not perfect?

Hosanna, Hosanna

When Christ rose Sunday morning after Simon's party, He knew that history had turned a corner. Mary's act of love had triggered Judas's latent hatred; events had been put in motion that would soon culminate in the grand showdown between good and evil, light and darkness, life and death. Jesus sets out on foot with His disciples for Jerusalem, no doubt following the same path that Judas had taken only hours before on the way to his midnight tryst with the Sanhedrin.

It is time now to turn the eyes of the world upon the Lamb of God. The roads are swollen with travelers heading to Jerusalem for the Passover Feast. Excitement builds as they realize that the renowned Teacher and Healer is in their midst. This time Christ does not discourage their attention. He does not slip away. He sends two disciples ahead for a colt. It is draped with cloaks, and He mounts it. The crowd goes wild. At last they will have their king! "Hosanna to the Son of David! . . . Hosanna in the highest!" they cry as they spread the road with palm branches. "Blessed is the King who comes in the name of the Lord! Peace in heaven and glory in the highest!" The crowd shouts in adoration. The religious leaders push their way through the noisy throng to Jesus, "Teacher, rebuke Your disciples," they demand sharply over the din.

Any way you look at the event, it's not good. The Romans have been pretty tolerant of religious festivals up to this point, but they might not be so tolerant of a coronation. Not to mention the fact that all hopes of dealing quietly and discretely with this upstart rabbi seem to be slipping quickly away as the crowd swells. "If they keep quiet the stones will cry out," Jesus calmly replies. The leaders will not be able to keep this event quiet. As much as they would like to, they will not be able to shroud His death in secrecy. What happens will be lifted up for all to see. Behold the King of the Jews. Behold the Son of God. Behold the Creator and Ruler of the universe. Behold the Lamb of God. Hosanna in the highest! (See Matthew 21 and Luke 19.)

THOUGHTS TO PONDER

❀ Why was it important that Christ's death be such a public event?

❀ What might have been the impact on history if the Pharisees had been able to assassinate Christ privately?

"Without God there is for mankind no purpose, no goal, no hope, only a wavering future, an eternal dread of every darkness."—Jean Paul

SING A NEW PSALM

The Psalms are a collection of public and private prayers. They are remarkable in their range of emotions and topics as well as for their honesty. They represent a dialog with God through good times and bad, through happiness and sorrow, through trust and doubt. Set aside a few minutes to write a prayer in the form of a psalm. Pick a subject for your psalm about something you are experiencing right now, or select one of the following topics:

A Psalm of Adoration	A Psalm of Praise	A Psalm of Sorrow
A Psalm of Glory	A Psalm of Repentance	A Psalm of Thanksgiving
A Psalm of Hope	A Psalm of Disappointment	A Psalm of Loss
A Psalm of Righteousness	A Psalm of Struggle	A Psalm of Peace

If you find this is a rewarding and meaningful form of worship, you may wish to keep a private journal of psalms, or you may wish to share your psalm with your family or study group. Try writing a group psalm. Sometimes we rush so fast through our prayers that it is a rewarding experience to consider in advance what we really want to say to God.

Mother Hen

As Christ, astride the donkey, rounded the bend at the top of the Mount of Olives, He came to a halt overlooking Jerusalem in the morning sun. The crowd cheered wildly, shouting hosannas and waving palm branches. Looking down upon the capital, Jesus heard their cheers reverberating throughout the valley and echoing off the city walls. They were so happy. They had no comprehension of the great cosmic battle being played out before them. The people just wanted a king to rescue them from the Romans. They wanted to feel a surge of patriotic pride for their homeland. They wanted the good old days again. They wanted Jesse's son. Instead, it was the Son of God who sat on a donkey in front of them. He could not give them what they wanted, an earthly king, because He was not of this earth. They would not accept what He had to offer, a cross and a crown of thorns, because they did not wish for salvation. They wanted only political clout. The two were at cross-purposes. Their hopes would be dashed and their hard lives made harder. If only they would let Him protect them. If only they could understand.

"As he approached Jerusalem and saw the city, he wept over it and said, 'If you, even you, had only known on this day what would bring you peace' " (Luke 19:41, 42).

"O Jerusalem, Jerusalem, you who kill the prophets and stone those sent to you, how often I have longed to gather your children together, as a hen gathers her chicks under her wings, but you were not willing!" (Luke 13:34).

MOUSSAKA
MIDDLE EASTERN ENTREE

This traditional Middle Eastern casserole calls for roasted vegetables to make a hearty and flavorful entree. Preparation time: 25 minutes. Baking time: 60 minutes plus 10 minutes to rest before serving. Serves 12-15.

Pantry Items
Garbanzos (2 15-oz. cans, drained and rinsed)
Crushed tomatoes (1 28-oz. can)
Olive oil (1 cup)
Coarse salt (1 Tbsp.)
Garlic salt (1 tsp.)

Fresh Items
2 Medium eggplants
(appoximately 12 cups cubed)
2 Medium onions (cut into 8 wedges each)
Fresh button mushrooms (8 oz. or 2 cups)
Fresh basil (2 Tbsp., chopped)
Ricotta cheese (2 cups)

DIRECTIONS
Preheat oven to 400° F. In a large bowl, gently toss cubed eggplant, onion wedges, and whole mushrooms with olive oil and coarse salt. Pour into 4-quart casserole baking dish. Roast vegetables for about 40 minutes or until they are fork tender and slightly browned. Turn vegetables gently with a metal spatula after 20 minutes. Meanwhile, mix garlic salt and ricotta cheese. Remove casserole from oven and add drained garbanzos, chopped basil, and crushed tomatoes to casserole. Mix in gently with roasted vegetables. Sprinkle ricotta evenly over the top of the casserole. If serving immediately, lower oven temperature to 350° F and bake until bubbling in middle and ricotta is starting to brown, approximately 20 to 25 minutes. If preparing for later, let casserole cool; cover with foil and refrigerate. Bring casserole to room temperature and remove foil before reheating. When finished baking, the moussaka should be allowed to rest for at least 10 minutes before serving.

Fire and Rain

Monday morning Jesus made His way to the temple. His time was short, and there was so much to say. The temple courtyard had been transformed into a crowded bazaar, catering to the Passover crowd. For the second time in three short years, Jesus cleared the temple of the moneychangers and merchants. No one opposed Him—not the bankers, not the hawkers of wares, not the temple guard, not even the priests. They all fled in panic at the sound of His voice, leaving their money and wares behind them. The Son of God had returned to His Father's house. No mortal man could oppose Him. When the priests finally plucked up the courage to sneak back to see what was happening, they found Jesus tenderly healing the sick and teaching the people. Little children were crowding around Him, singing songs. He hardly looked like a menacing anarchist. Feeling furious and a little foolish at their cowardice, the priests demanded to know by what authority Jesus had taken over the temple, but they were not so sure of themselves as to demand that He leave. In fact, Jesus returned the next day and the next. The Lamb of God Himself presided over the last Passover. Helpless to stop Him, the priests tried to trick Him with contrived questions, but Christ turned the mockery back on the questioners and heaped condemnation upon them. They had robbed, abused, and beaten down the people. They had done it in the name of the Father. The Son had come to set the record straight. These corrupt leaders did not represent a loving God!

As His time in the temple finally drew to a close, Christ knew that He had done all He could to minister to the people, to give them a foundation, a base for hope for the dark days that lay ahead. But for most it would not be enough. Christ lifted up His hands to the heavens: "Now My heart is troubled, and what shall I say? 'Father, save Me from this hour'? No, it was for this very reason I came to this hour. Father, glorify Your name!" The voice of God thundered back, "I have glorified it, and will glorify it again." (See John 12:27, 28.) Christ passed from the temple. Some had received fiery condemnation. Some had received showers of blessing. Some had heard the voice of God.

THOUGHTS TO PONDER

❀ If I profess to be a Christian, how important is the way I live my life and conduct my affairs?

❀ Will Christ hold me accountable for how well or poorly I present God through my actions?

BIBLE VILLAGE
INSIDE ACTIVITY

Ages: 1st Grade to Adult
Materials Needed:
   Small empty cardboard boxes such as individual-size cereal boxes,
      pasta boxes, or cosmetic/medicine boxes
   Brown craft paper or brown paper bags
   Clear tape
   Markers or tempera paint
   Play-Doh modeling compound

This is an inexpensive craft project that your kids will really enjoy. You probably have most of the items on hand already. You may need to plan ahead and save small cardboard boxes for a few weeks until you have collected enough boxes to create a small Bible village. Help your children wrap the boxes as you would wrap a gift with brown paper and clear tape. Encourage them to draw or paint arched doors and windows on the boxes, using black paint or markers. Arrange the decorated boxes into a village. Use the Play-Doh to make palm trees, animals, and people. Populate the village with characters or animals from a favorite Bible story or current Sabbath School lesson.

Holy Places and Viper Dens

The sanctuary was not designed by human beings. Its blueprint was dictated by God for the children of Israel in the wilderness. It was a divine shadow play, an object lesson, an enactment of the plan of salvation. God wanted to make the sacrifice and atonement for sin so clear that everyone could understand it. But by the time Jesus walked the earth, the meaning of the sanctuary rituals had sunk into obscurity. The Jews believed, much as their pagan neighbors did, that it was necessary to appease the wrath of an angry God with blood and ritual. The clergy exercised enormous control over everyday activities and skimmed a commission off nearly every transaction. The plan designed by God to provide ongoing spiritual guidance for the people had been turned into a corrupt racket, milking the people it was designed to serve.

Before we become too indignant with the priests and the Pharisees, we should probably consider that we don't have to look far to observe religious tyranny in our time. The ring of power is as seductive and corrupting today as it was in Jesus' time. Christ reserved His most scathing criticisms for the religious leaders. What would He have to say to us today? To stand between God and His people is to stand on dangerous ground.

THOUGHTS TO PONDER
- At the Resurrection we became a priesthood of believers. What responsibility does that entail?
- Do I encourage my children to analyze what they are taught, or does analysis and evaluation frighten me?

"And of all plagues with which mankind are cursed / Ecclesiastic tyranny's the worst."
—Daniel Defoe

PLANNING A GARDEN

Armchair gardening is great fun! Whether you have an acre or just a few square yards to work with, planning the garden is one of the best parts of having a garden. All you need to get started is a pad of graph paper, a seed catalog, and a map of temperature zones available in nearly all gardening books or online at <www.growit.com/ZONES>.

Growing Areas: To grow a garden you need to meet at least three important criteria:

❀ No danger of frost (check temperate zone maps for outside planting guides).
❀ A minimum of 5 to 6 hours of sunlight a day (mark off during weekends if you're not sure).
❀ Rich, drainable soil. (This can be in a garden plot, a raised bed, or a container.)

Mrs. Lois Burpee, of the famous Burpee seed family, recommended planting very modest vegetable gardens, much to her husband's dismay. He complained that "you're not helping me to sell seeds." I have to agree with Mrs. Burpee. When it comes to vegetable gardens, less is less work, and less can still be plenty. Mrs. Burpee makes the following recommendations for a garden for a family of four: six tomato plants, two zucchini plants, and three pepper plants.

My personal recommendation would be slightly different: six tomato plants of different varieties, two cucumber plants, one squash plant, one zucchini plant, and two pepper plants. You may have noticed that all these plants are climbing plants and can be grown in a small area if you install trellis or growing cages for them to climb on. You know your family's personal favorites best. What kind of vegetable garden would they enjoy? If you keep it simple, you are sure to find that a vegetable garden of a very modest size will reap big flavor dividends throughout the summer and early fall.

The Good, the Bad, and the Ugly

One of the most haunting images I have seen was a piece of newsreel footage of Mother Teresa in Calcutta. Mother Teresa had come to visit a local hospital. Crowds of people thronged the tiny woman as she made her way slowly through the courtyard. She walked with both palms turned outward, caressing faces, hands, and shoulders as she walked. Grown men, small children, weeping women—all who came close received the same gentle touch. She looked so unhurried, so focused on the faces in front of her. The news cameras followed her into the hospital halls. The crowds were behind her now. On the bare cots lay dozens of sick and dying men, women, and children. Bodies covered in open sores, disfigured faces, amputated limbs. My eyes squinted as I watched; it was painful to look at. Thousands of miles away in the comfort of my own living room, I involuntarily cringed at the revulsion of decaying flesh. Mother Teresa did not. She approached each cot as if the occupant were her beloved child. She stroked their faces, smoothed their hair, examined their wounds, and cradled their poor broken bodies in her arms.

If Christians represent the body of Christ on this earth, I believe Mother Teresa exemplified God's hands. That is how I picture Christ as He taught and healed in the temple courtyard during the last week before His crucifixion. As the temple priests no doubt drew their robes about them in disgust, the sick, the dying, and the maimed thronged about Christ. I can see Christ's hands touching, caressing, healing. No disfigurement so revolting, no wound so infected, no disease so terminal, that it could not be cured by the Life-Giver. The unholy and the unclean were restored with forgiveness and healing. Only the "good," with their self-righteousness robes wrapped tightly about them, could not experience the healing touch of the hand of God.

THOUGHTS TO PONDER

- How can I be the "hands of God" for those in need?
- Can I submit my life humbly to the healing power of the Savior?

"One's life has value so long as one attributes value to the life of others, by means of love, friendship, indignation and compassion." —Simone De Beauvoir

THE HANDS OF GOD

It is our privilege and responsibility to carry out the work of God on earth. Not all of us can devote our lives to the care of the poor and the sick, but we can all lend a helping hand. Examine your time and your resources. How can you get personally involved? Would you be able to involve your whole family or study group in a service project? Consider some of the following avenues of service:

❀ Donate some time at your local church community service center.
❀ Organize an Adopt-a-Grandparent program at an assisted living facility.
❀ Share time in a local soup kitchen.
❀ Start a sandwich ministry for the homeless.
❀ Train to be a volunteer at a local hospital or hot line.
❀ Develop personal care packages for women in crisis.
❀ Collect secondhand suits for emerging career women.

Thirty Pieces of Silver

The story of Judas is a puzzle. Two thousand years after his death, religious and secular authors are still trying to divine the motivation behind Judas's betrayal. It would have been one thing if an assassin had been paid thirty pieces of silver to ambush Christ in the middle of the night. History would have reviled such a monster. But Judas was part of the inner circle surrounding Christ. For three years Judas ate, slept, and walked with the greatest Prophet/Healer ever to arise out of Israel. Of that at least he must have been sure, yet he agreed to lead the enemy to his Master in the dead of night. What tempted him into becoming the world's most infamous betrayer? Was it the money? Thirty pieces of silver was undoubtedly a handsome sum. Did it all come down to greed? Does everyone have his price?

What was Judas's payoff if it wasn't greed? Some have speculated that it was revenge for imagined slights and rebuffs. The fact that Judas met with the priests just after Christ openly rebuked him at Simon's house lends some credence to that theory. Others suggest that Judas never expected the Healer/Teacher to allow Himself to be hurt and just wanted to give the reluctant rabbi a push toward His destiny. After all, Judas had seen Him raise the dead; was Christ really in any danger? Another speculation is that Christ provoked Judas to betray Him because He needed to die to save the world. Was Christ so lacking in enemies that He needed to manipulate a disciple into doing the dirty deed? That doesn't seem to have been the case. For whatever reason, Judas made a fateful decision on the night of Simon's party. He, a little nobody, a lackey, a whipping boy, wound up in a clandestine meeting in the dead of night with the nation's most elite group of powerbrokers. He was there to negotiate a deal. He had their attention. They agreed to his terms. Soon he would have the attention of Christ. Who would be the whipping boy then? "By his wounds we are healed" (Isaiah 53:5).

THOUGHTS TO PONDER
❀ Isn't it easy to feel angry when other church members don't recognize my real importance?
❀ Isn't it difficult to keep remembering that it's not about me, but all about Christ?

"Self-confidence is either a petty pride in our own narrowness, or the realization of our duty and privilege as God's children."— Phillips Brooks, American minister and poet, 1835-1893

A VISION AND A MISSION

Every day we make choices based on our mission in life. We commit our time, our money, and our creative energy into supporting our personal vision, whether we have clearly defined that vision or not. Have you thought about what your life mission is? Have you developed a personal vision statement? What are your central goals? What do you want to accomplish in life? Write your goals down in a vision statement. The next document you write could be a mission statement. A mission statement is an outline of how you hope to achieve your vision. Dr. Stephen Covey, in his 1990 bestseller *The 7 Habits of Highly Effective People,* contends that all truly successful people have a clearly defined personal vision. What's yours? If you haven't already done so, take a little time to write yours down. Follow it up with a mission statement. Explain to yourself how you are going to achieve your personal vision. Keep your vision and mission statements where you can refer to them often.

Password

While Jesus taught openly in the temple courtyard during Passover, the priests and the Pharisees seethed. Their attempts to trick Him into making a damaging remark that would alienate the people or at least split His supporters had all backfired. They didn't need a political analyst to tell them that they were plummeting in the polls. Christ's blunt criticisms were rapidly undermining their authority. This upstart rabbi needed to be eliminated before all their authority was lost. "Better . . . that one man die for the people than that the whole nation perish," warned Caiaphas, the designated high priest (John 11:50). They wanted to wait until after the Passover crowds had left, but the situation was clearly out of control. More people were flocking to Jesus daily. He seemed to be openly mocking their authority. Tuesday afternoon the Jewish leaders called in their ace in the hole, Judas. They demanded that Judas deliver Jesus, preferably unarmed and alone, at the first opportunity.

But Christ, who understood and read all hearts, was not quite ready for this final chapter. He desired to perform one last act of service for His disciples. Christ made secret arrangements for their Passover meal. He didn't even entrust His closest disciples with an address. Judas would be given no opportunity to interrupt the important Last Supper with a "surprise." Instead, Peter and John were instructed to follow a man carrying a water jar on his head (rather an oddity in a culture where the women were the water bearers) to an unknown house. They were given a prearranged question to ask and told what answer to expect. A furnished room would be waiting for them. Peter and John were to prepare the Passover meal there, and Jesus would follow with the rest of the disciples when it was time. Why all the cloak-and-dagger activity complete with secret operatives, a safe house, and a password? Because John 13; 14; 15; and 16 had not yet been spoken; because Jesus desired to wash the disciples' feet; because on the eve of Gethsemane, Jesus was thinking of you and me. "Do this in remembrance of me" (Luke 22:19).

THOUGHTS TO PONDER
❀ Do I cherish my opportunities to perform the ordinance of humility with other believers?
❀ Christ went to great trouble to prepare a Communion service. Why is it important to me?

"It was pride that changed angels into devils; it is humility that makes men as angels."
—St. Augustine

CONFIDENTIALITY

Can you be trusted to keep a confidence? Few things are more hurtful than to be betrayed by a friend's carelessness. Still there are confidences that you shouldn't keep. What can you do? Consider the following guidelines the next time you are asked to keep a secret:

1. Never promise to keep a secret before you know what it is. Assure them that you will value and respect their trust, but you can make no promises. If they decide not to share, do not pry. Respect their privacy.
2. Never treat a confidence casually. Share information only if the actions put individuals at risk or are illegal. Report information only to appropriate authorities and involve the fewest individuals possible. Strive always to protect the interests and reputation of the confidante.
3. Behave in the manner of a good listener. Do not judge or criticize. Ask how they would like you to help them. Provide a safe place for them to discuss their problems and search for solutions.

Toiletries

Perhaps it was the stress or the excitement of the past week, but by the time Jesus arrived with the rest of the disciples to the upper room Thursday evening, everyone seemed to be in a mood. Peter and John had been hard at work all day preparing the Passover Feast and were undoubtedly tired. Judas had plenty on his mind to keep him preoccupied. The remaining nine were keenly aware that the situation between Jesus and the Jewish leaders had become so taut that something was bound to snap. It's not surprising that the air crackled with tension and that bickering broke out at the table. It sounds so childish and silly when you read it in the Bible: "A dispute arose among them as to which of them was considered to be greatest." Considered to be greatest by whom? What had any of them done to be considered great? Time was winding down. Jesus had only hours left to prepare the disciples for the darkest hour of their lives, and they were sniping and squabbling like schoolboys. Jesus needed their attention. He required the attention of their hearts. "So He got up from the meal, took off His outer clothing, and wrapped a towel around His waist. After that, He poured water into a basin and began to wash His disciples' feet, drying them with the towel that was wrapped around Him." The gentle point was lost on no one. Peter was stricken to the heart, ashamed and embarrassed as Christ gently bathed his dirty feet. "When He had finished washing their feet, He put on His clothes and returned to His place. 'Do you understand what I have done for you?' He asked them. 'You call Me "Teacher" and "Lord," and rightly so, for that is what I am. Now that I, your Lord and Teacher, have washed your feet, you also should wash one another's feet.'" He had their attention. (See Luke 22 and John 13.)

THOUGHTS TO PONDER
- Have you ever considered what might happen if Christ sat in on a church board meeting?
- Who won the last argument I was in? Does it matter?

"Jesus is the God whom we can approach without pride and before whom we can humble ourselves without despair."—Blaise Pascal, French mathematician, physicist, and philosopher, 1623-1662

FIGHT CLUB RULES

When spouses fight, there are no winners. But we would really like to win, wouldn't we? We want to prove our point, punish our foe, or establish our superiority. Losing isn't fun. It feels rotten. It leaves us frustrated, angry, and resentful. Does making our life partner feel like that really qualify as a win for us? Is winning so important that we can justify putting our marriages, our children, and our future at risk? If constant bickering is eroding your relationship, sit down with your spouse and discuss your options. After too many bruising verbal battles, my husband and I decided to at least agree upon the rules of the ring. These are our "Fight Club Rules":

1. One person speaks at a time. The other takes notes.
2. Before the second person speaks, he or she reads back the notes and allows the first person to correct any misconceptions.
3. When the second person speaks, the same rules apply.
4. If an agreement is reached, it is written down and signed off by both parties.
5. If an agreement isn't reached, the issue is a forbidden topic until another discussion can be scheduled.

If emotionally damaging fights are destroying your relationship, at least start by setting the "Fight Club Rules." You may find that you have a lot more common ground than you had thought.

Broken Bodies

As Christ breaks the Passover bread, He understands that soon He will be subjected to the pent-up fury of the temple leaders He has rebuked so soundly and publicly during the past week. He will endure the pain, but it will break His disciples' hearts. In spite of their petty bickering, He knows that they love Him. He wants to give them something to hang on to. He wants to help them understand that as bad as it is going to get, He has chosen this path. "I am telling you now before it happens, so that when it does happen you will believe that I am He." The disciples are confused and nervous. What is He talking about? "I tell you the truth, one of you is going to betray Me." They believe Him. His words carry a deep conviction. They are dumbstruck. Which one? Christ takes a loaf of bread in His strong hands. "I tell you the truth, one of you will betray Me—one who is eating with Me." Peter quickly motions to John to ask whom Jesus is talking about. "Is it I?" they inquire one by one. Jesus bows His head in blessing over the bread. His fingers deliberately break it into pieces. He hands it toward His disciples. "Take and eat; this is My body." Then dipping the piece of bread, He hands it to Judas Iscariot. "Surely not I, Rabbi?" Judas asks with hands uplifted to receive the broken loaf. Christ holds Judas's inquiring gaze in His and replies, "It is as you say." Was it a question or a statement? Was it Judas's last chance? Judas takes the bread from Christ's hand without a reply. Satan enters into him now. There will be no turning back. "What you are about to do, do quickly," Jesus instructs. "As soon as Judas had taken the bread, he went out. And it was night." Before the sun sets again, one will be hanged—the other crucified. (See Matthew 26; Mark 14; and John 13.)

THOUGHT TO PONDER

❀ Is it possible that God might want to tell me something that I am not willing to understand?

PASSOVER PLATTER
POCKET SANDWICHES

The following meal of flat bread, spreads, dips, and vegetables is still served in the Middle East today. The ingredients can be carried to potluck and arranged on site. Preparation time: 10 minutes. Serves 6.

Pantry Items
Olive oil (1 cup)
Black and green olives

Fresh Items
Pita bread or other flat bread (6 slices)
Tabouli (1 container or see Week 11, Friday)
Pita chips (1 bag) optional
Hummus dip (1 container)
Feta cheese or other soft cheese (1 container)
Mixed baby salad greens (1 package)
Cucumber (1)
Onion (1)

DIRECTIONS

Peel and slice cucumber and onion. Cut pita and/or flat bread into half or quarters (depending whether you want to dip the bread or use the bread to make sandwiches). Pour the olive oil into a salad dressing carafe. Set the tabouli, hummus, and cheese in small serving bowls. Arrange the rest of the ingredients around the bowls on a large platter or tray. Drizzle a little olive oil over the cheese and veggies and set the remainder aside to be passed.

Bleeding Hearts

The mood around the table has turned somber. Judas has been sent off on an errand. The Lord is not His usual self. He's talking about betrayal. Perhaps He is angry with them for bickering earlier. Perhaps He means *betray* in a symbolic sense. Perhaps they have all betrayed Him. They have all at least disappointed Him. Christ has blessed and broken the bread, "Take and eat; this is My body." Now He holds up the wine. "This cup is the new covenant in My blood, which is poured out for you." He drinks of the cup, then passes it around the table, and they all drink. They don't understand. "My children, I will be with you only a little longer. . . . Where I am going, you cannot come." What does He mean? Their souls fill with apprehension. Peter can't stand it. "Lord, why can't I follow You now? I will lay down my life for You."

"Peter, Peter, before dawn you will disown Me three times." Peter's heart is broken. He is the betrayer? The Master meant him? Christ looks into his eyes. "Do not let your heart be troubled. Peter, I tell you that you will deny Me, but try to remember, Trust in God; trust also in Me." Peter hears the words, but they do not make any sense. The Master is leaving? Jesus expects Peter to let Him down? Why? Where is He going? "In My Father's house are many rooms; if it were not so, I would have told you. I am going to prepare a place for you. Peter, listen to Me; you will be with Me. I will come back and take you to be with Me that you also may be where I am. I will not abandon you, even if you abandon Me. You know the way to the place where I am going. Don't let your heart be troubled, Peter. I am the Way and the Truth and the Life." (See Matthew 26; Luke 22; and John 13; 14.)

THOUGHT TO PONDER

❀ Can I accept the fact God still loves and wants me even when I have let Him down?

FINGER PUPPETS
INSIDE ACTIVITY

Ages: Preschoolers
Materials Needed:
    Felt-tip pen
    Cotton balls
    Coated rubber bands
    Small fabric scraps (5 x 5 inches)
    Ribbon

This is an extremely simple activity, but my preschoolers loved it and would beg me to do it with them every Sabbath. I bet yours will too! On Sabbath afternoon, we would open the Sabbath School Quarterly to the lesson they had just reviewed in Sabbath School. They would pick the Bible characters they wanted to play, and I would draw a smiley face (just the eyes and the mouth) on their fingertip with a felt-tip pen. If the character was an old man, we would attach a cotton ball just below the eyes with a rubber band to make a fluffy gray beard. If it was a younger man, we would attach a fabric scrap with a rubber band above the face like an Arab kaffiyeh (headdress). If it was a woman, we draped the fabric over the finger and slipped the rubber band below the face. Babies and little children just got a few curls drawn with the felt-tip pen. Sometimes the children had two or three characters on each hand, and we would reenact the Sabbath School lesson together. Playing finger puppets is a great way to review the lesson. You'd be surprised at how much the little ones remember! Remember to remove all rubber bands and wash their fingers when the play is over.

Note: Please make sure your little ones are at least three years old—old enough to keep from putting their fingers in their mouths—and that the rubber bands are not on too tight!

Bitter Herbs

Bitter herbs are part of the Passover Seder. They symbolize the bitter tribulation of the children of Israel under the whips of their Egyptian masters. Israel was always to celebrate their freedom while remembering their slavery. So it was on the last Passover. The blood of the Lamb of God would set the world free. Yet the Lamb would grieve for those who would not be freed, for those He could not save.

As Christ implores the Father to protect His small flock during the coming storm, He remembers the one who has already been lost. The one he could not save. The one he can no longer protect. "While I was with them, I protected them and kept them safe by that name You gave Me. None has been lost except the one doomed to destruction." "Woe to that man who betrays the Son of Man! It would be better for him if he had not been born." Jesus knows that as He speaks, the betrayer is preparing to lead an armed expedition to rendezvous with them in the olive groves when the night is deep, the campfires are extinguished, and good men sleep. When he arrives, Christ will have one last opportunity—a few split seconds—to reach for the heart of the one who is lost. He will be waiting. (See Matthew 26 and John 17.)

THOUGHTS TO PONDER
- ❊ Am I capable of grieving for the loss of my enemies?
- ❊ Are there ones whom I love that I feel powerless to help? Do I believe that God has not given up on them?

"Through pride we are ever deceiving ourselves. But deep down below the surface of the average conscience a still, small voice says to us, Something is out of tune."—Carl Jung

HERB GARDENS

If you've ever seen an herb garden, you've probably dreamed of starting one of your own. The small aromatic plants were often beautifully laid out in geometric beds beside colonial kitchens. Sometimes they were used as borders for flowerbeds. Like regular gardens, herbs need five to six hours of sunlight; good, drainable soil; and a temperate environment. But because of their comparatively compact size, herbs can be grown in almost any small nook with the above requirements. The first herb garden I saw was arranged in containers on stepladders on a tiny seaside patio in Florida. In spite of the intense sun and salt air, the herb garden thrived behind carefully placed windscreens. In some places, herb gardens can be grown in the summer just outside the kitchen door. You've probably seen, as I have, kitchen herb gardens in a "bump out" window or under grow lights. Thinking of planting your own herb garden?

- ❊ **Sweet Basil or Lemon Basil.** This popular "pesto herb" is found in many Asian and Mediterranean dishes. The plant is easy to grow in the garden among the flowers or in a container. Pinch off any flowers, or the plant will get too spindly.
- ❊ **Parsley, Flat or Curly.** This popular herb, used to season potatoes, salads, and casseroles, can be planted as a border or in pots. Parsley likes to spread out, but it can be kept clipped back with use. The plant will continue to grow back for the season if the thickest stem in the middle is left.
- ❊ **Mint.** Perfect for iced tea and lemonade, mint leaves are also used in many Indian and Middle Eastern recipes. Mint can be grown easily in containers as well as in the garden.
- ❊ **Thyme.** Used in savory dishes such as stews, casseroles, and dressings, this herb is another that grows well in containers.
- ❊ **Rosemary.** This herb is used in Mediterranean and savory dishes, such as soups and stews. A woody herb that can grow to the size of a small shrub, rosemary does well in a large clay pot that can be brought in before the frost and watered during the winter.

Lean on Me

After Judas leaves the upper room, Jesus turns His full attention to the remaining eleven disciples. In just a few hours, the very roots of their faith will be shaken. They are still spiritually weak, but if they will just let Him, He will pull them through this difficult experience. "I am going away," He tells them. "Where are You going, Lord?" Peter wants to know. He believes he is brave. He is prepared to die for Christ. But his job is not to be a deliverer. His job tonight is to be a witness, and Peter is not strong enough for that.

"You will deny Me three times before dawn, Peter, but let not your heart be troubled. I know you, Peter, but all you have to do is trust Me."

"How will we find You if You go without us?" Thomas worries. "We don't know where You are going."

"I know you think I will abandon you, Thomas, but I am the path to safety. I am the Way, the Truth, and the Life. If you know Me, you know God. Trust Me, Thomas."

Philip wants more concrete answers. It sounds like riddles to him. "Lord, show us the Father, and that will be enough for us."

"Oh, Philip, after all this time, don't you know Me? If you have seen Me, you have seen the Father. How can you say, 'Show us the Father'? Believe Me when I say We are one, or if you can't believe that, at least believe on the evidence of the miracles. Ask anything in My name, Philip, and I will do it. You know I can; you've seen the evidence."

Which brings the other Judas (not Judas Iscariot) to the burning question on all of their minds. "Do You intend to make Yourself known just to us and not to the world?" They are having such a hard time letting go of their idea of the mighty Prophet-King. Visions of cheering crowds, marching armies, a kingdom of righteousness such as the world has never seen is slipping like sand through their fingers. Why is Jesus going away now? Why doesn't Jesus just show the people who He really is? Jesus draws a deep breath. They will be scattered like sheep without a shepherd. "I am going away, but I will send the Holy Spirit to you. He is sort of like a counselor. He will help you understand." Jesus rises. The prince of this world is coming. The hour is late. There are no more delays. "Come now," He says, "let us leave." (See Matthew 26; John 16; 17.)

THOUGHTS TO PONDER
- ❀ Am I sometimes apprehensive about the future?
- ❀ Can I rest in the faith that Christ will pull me through if I trust Him to, even if I am not strong?

"Faith makes a Christian. Life proves a Christian. Trial confirms a Christian.
Death crowns a Christian."—Author Unknown

LIFELINES

Surviving a spiritual failure or crisis is tough. We believe we've let our friends, our church, and our family down. We have let Jesus down. We feel ashamed that we weren't stronger. If you have been through a spiritual crisis or you know of someone who has, refer to John, chapters 14-17, the conversation that Jesus had with His disciples just before they all deserted Him in Gethsemane. Christ throws out several lifelines to His disciples for their upcoming spiritual crisis. The lifelines are still here for us today.

❀ Christ knew we would let Him down, yet He still loves us just as He loved Peter. John 14:1-3, "Let not your heart be troubled," was spoken to Peter just after Jesus predicted that Peter would deny Him.
❀ Jesus has sent the Holy Spirit to guide and comfort us. He will bring us back into a true relationship with Christ.
❀ We are invited to ask anything in the name of Jesus. Over and over again, Jesus encourages His disciples to call on the Father in His name.
❀ We are to love one another and encourage one another in our time of need, as Christ has loved us.

The Flesh Is Weak

All the way from the upper room in Jerusalem to the Garden of Gethsemane, Jesus talks to and encourages His disciples. He assures them of His love and the Father's love. He answers question after question, even questions they haven't asked yet. Finally, they think they've got it. "We understand You at last," they tell Him. "You are answering questions we haven't even asked yet. This makes us believe that You came from God."

I have to believe that Christ must have laughed. "You believe at last," He replies with a smile. But His smile soon fades because He knows too well that they don't really know what they believe. "Soon you will be scattered each to his own house. You will leave Me alone. But I will not be alone," He assures them. He wants them to know this when they bitterly despise themselves for running away. "My Father is with Me. I am telling you these things so you may have peace."

Jesus raises His face to the heavens and prays, "Father, the time has come. . . ." His prayer is a glorious love song to the Father, a prayer of love for His disciples, a prayer of love for those who are yet to come. Standing on the precipice of Gethsemane, Christ looks down the centuries to you and me and lifts us up before the Father in prayer. "Because You loved Me," He tells the Father, "before the creation of the world . . ." With the end of the prayer, Christ's tender ministry to His disciples comes to an end. His spirit grows dark. The blackness has begun to press in upon Him. The disciples cannot see what is troubling Him. "My soul is overwhelmed with sorrow to the point of death," He tells them. "Stay and pray with Me," He entreats them. But like small children after an exhausting day, they nod off, in spite of their best intentions. The spirit is willing but the flesh is so very weak. (See John 16 and 17.)

THOUGHTS TO PONDER

❀ If I had been at Gethsemane, would I have been able to stay awake and comfort Christ?

❀ Do I sometimes, even with the benefit of historical perspective, take Jesus' sacrifice for granted?

"I live in company with a body, a silent companion, exacting and eternal. He it is who notes that individuality which is the seal of the weakness of our race. My soul has wings, but the brutal jailer is strict."—Eugène Delacroix, artist

AGE-APPROPRIATE BEHAVIORS

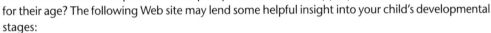

Before we become parents, we are all certain that we will not be one of those parents who allow their children to grow up spoiled and out of control, but that is before we become parents. Real parenting is a process of working with a child's natural development. It would be ridiculous to expect a newborn to go through potty training. It is equally unsatisfactory to demand that a toddler sit quietly. How can we as parents work patiently with our children to help them develop responsible behavior appropriate for their age? The following Web site may lend some helpful insight into your child's developmental stages:

❀ **www.childdevelopmentinfo.com**
   This great Web site offers a wide range of information on children's mental, physical, and emotional development. This site also provides book reviews on a wide range of parenting and child-development topics.

Anguish

Much has been written about Gethsemane. But the hard truth is that we don't really understand exactly what caused Christ to sweat blood and fall to the ground in anguish. Was He wrestling with the idea of death? As God, didn't He know that He would rise triumphant? Was He anticipating the cruel torture that was going to be inflicted on Him, the multiple beatings, the crown of thorns, the nails on the cross? Was He fighting to bring His divine powers into submission, to refrain from annihilating His torturers? Was His heart breaking as He accepted the evil of the world upon Himself and as God withdrew from Him? We are of this earth and cannot see or comprehend the forces that would bring an Almighty God to His knees in sacrifice for us.

The defining battle of time and eternity was played out between Gethsemane and Golgotha. But we can see only the wounds inflicted during the cosmic struggle and not the battle itself. Christ, who had been so tenderly focused on His disciples' welfare just a short time earlier, falls prostrate on the ground, pleading with God to find some other way. He cries out "Abba . . . Daddy!" But the Father does not answer. This time there is no thundering reply from the heavens. The Bible says the disciples don't know what to say to Him. They see only a solitary man in anguish. They can see nothing else. Again Christ begs the Father, "Take this cup from Me." What is Christ wrestling with? He is being crushed under its weight. Great drops of sweat and blood seep from His brow and run down His face. "Thy will be done," He gasps and collapses. He has fully acquiesced to whatever unimaginable horrors can cause a God to sweat blood. An angel is sent to revive Him. Men appear to be totally useless at this point. Christ has survived the first round. Whatever wounds He has sustained are not visible. He walks calmly over to the disciples. "Are you still sleeping and resting?" He asks in disbelief. "Enough! The hour has come." (See Matthew 26 and John 17.)

THOUGHTS TO PONDER
- What happened to Christ in the Garden of Gethsemane?
- Is it possible that we, like the disciples, will sleep up until the final hours of the great controversy?

"The Christian ideal has not been tried and found wanting. It has been found difficult; and left untried."—G. K. Chesterton, 1874–1936

GRIEF RECOVERY

There are moments in everyone's life when they experience grief or loss so profound that it feels as if they will be crushed under the weight of it, that they cannot possibly go on living. Life on a sinful planet is an extended series of losses. We loose parents, siblings, friends, lovers, sometimes even children, long before we are ready. Grief is a process we are all forced to participate in. But there is help available for our aching hearts.

❀ *Understanding Grief, Helping Yourself Heal* by Dr. Alan D. Wolfelt is a compassionate and practical guide to dealing with loss. You may also want to visit his Web site: <www.centerforloss.com> for additional resources available for grieving individuals and families.

❀ *The Grief Recovery Handbook: The Action Program for Moving Beyond Death, Divorce, and Other Losses,* by John W. James and Russell Friedman is a step-by-step process for dealing with loss, whether through death or divorce.

❀ *A Grief Observed* by C. S. Lewis is an intimate journey through grief by one of the twentieth century's most influential Christian writers. A spiritually thought-provoking and moving experience.

Kiss of Death

The night is dark as Judas leads the hastily assembled detachment of temple guards and ruffians along the narrow, winding streets of Jerusalem, past the city gates, and through the hills and fields toward Gethsemane. As they wind deeper and deeper into the ancient groves, the light from the lanterns and torches seems to fade into the night air. The men clutch their swords and clubs and curse the darkness, straining to keep their eyes on the man in front of them. What is Judas thinking? Is he having second thoughts, or is his ambitious heart pumping with adrenalin as he pushes forward into the night, hoping that Jesus will be at the same familiar, secluded spot tonight. In his mind he pictures the surprise on Jesus' face. He, Judas, will feign confusion and bewilderment as if he has just stumbled upon this wild mob on his way back to camp. He will rush to Jesus' side in a show of support, as if to embrace Him with a kiss. This is the sign.

What does he imagine will happen next? Does Judas imagine that the band of thugs will lead Jesus and the rest of the disciples off in shackles, or does he imagine that Jesus will spring into action to rescue Himself and the others? Does Judas believe that an armed threat will finally force Jesus to publicly declare Himself the Messiah, or has Judas become disillusioned with this Messiah's prospects? Either way, it is a terrible risk. At any point it could go terribly wrong for Judas. Judas must believe that he is smart enough to play both ends against the middle and win no matter what happens. But nothing goes according to plan. Jesus is awake and waiting for Judas. There is no surprise. As Judas rushes forward in mock surprise, Jesus quietly focuses His attention on Judas, not on the armed men. "My friend, what are you doing?" Jesus inquires quietly. Judas is not expecting this response, but it is too late. He pushes forward to embrace Him. "Would you betray the Son of Man with a kiss?" Christ pointedly asks. Last chance, my friend . . . but it is too late; Judas cannot turn back now. Even though he knows Jesus knows, he kisses Him anyway. It is the kiss of death. God is not fooled. (See Luke 22.)

THOUGHTS TO PONDER

❀ Have I ever started down a path that I knew was wrong but didn't seem to be able to stop?

❀ Could Christ have forgiven Judas even after he had betrayed Him?

"The last temptation is the greatest treason: To do the right deed for the wrong reason."
—T. S. Eliot

SPIRITUAL GIFTS AND BESETTING SINS

The Bible is full of stories of gifted men such as Judas who have abused their God-given gifts and talents. Any gift or talent not submitted to God's direction can easily become our besetting sin. What are your gifts and talents? Have you submitted them to God? If you're not sure, set aside some time for the following exercise in gift discernment:

1. Make a list of six or seven activities or accomplishments that you really enjoyed and that you know you did well. List only those experiences that were both enjoyable and successful.
2. Now list the talents and skills you employed in those activities. Were your skills in building, organizing, helping, persuading, creating, leading, teaching, etc.?
3. Pay particular attention to the skills and talents that reoccur repeatedly. Those are your special gifts. You are particularly motivated to use those skills and to use them well. In fact, you are probably tempted to exercise those gifts even when it is not appropriate.
4. Trust that God has a purpose for those gifts and will not allow them to languish. Dedicate those special skills to God. Understand that God may choose not to use them at times. Your gifts, sanctified by God's direction, will take wings and soar beyond your wildest dreams. It is what you were created for.

Hero Worship

When Judas brushes the Master's face with his lips, good and evil embrace—and all hell breaks loose. The armed men rush toward Jesus and His small band of followers. "Whom do you seek?" the Master asks, clearly unafraid. Not expecting the question, the mob pauses to answer Him, "We want Jesus of Nazareth." "I am He," Jesus replies. Even as He speaks, Jesus drops the veil of His mortality, and His revealed glory sends the men reeling backward. It is the great "I Am," Jehovah, who stands before them. There must be no mistake, no innocent bystanders. "Whom do you seek?" Jesus asks again as the men lie at His feet. He is Himself now, just a man. The men spring to their feet. "Jesus of Nazareth," they scream. They have been tricked. They seize Christ. "I told you I am He, let these men go," Jesus replies. The disciples have been awakened by the mob. For a moment Jesus seems to have the situation well in hand, but then they see the mob charge and overwhelm Him. They spring into action. "Lord, should we strike with our swords?" Peter bellows for the benefit of the rest. Already his weapon is crashing down upon the captors. Whether it is the dim light, a sudden movement, or poor aim, the heavy sword misses its mark and cleaves Malchus's ear, not his skull. First blood has been drawn. Christ spins toward Peter. "Enough!" He commands. "Do you not think I could call on twelve legions of angels? Am I not to drink the cup the Father has given Me?" Christ reaches for His captor's injured ear and restores it. It is too much for the disciples to comprehend! Their Champion has surrendered. Still groggy, now confused and terrified, the disciples scatter in all directions. Christ addresses the mob. He knows these men. They have been eyeing Him belligerently from behind temple columns and courtyard corners for three days, unable to lay a hand on Him. "Am I leading an armed rebellion that you need swords and clubs to capture Me? Why didn't you arrest Me in the temple courts?" He taunts. The full attention of their malice is focused squarely on Him. "But this is your hour—when darkness reigns." The men angrily grab the hands that have so recently healed Malchus's ear and bind them behind His back. His disciples slip safely into the darkness. (See Mark 14; Luke 22; and John 18.)

THOUGHT TO PONDER

❊ Is it possible that sometimes when I feel God has abandoned me that He is protecting me?

VEGETABLE KOFTAS WITH YOGURT DIP
MIDDLE EASTERN APPETIZER

These spicy lentil-nut balls are prepared using many foods mentioned in the Bible. Preparation time: 25 minutes. Cooking time: 20 minutes. Baking time: 15-20 minutes. Serves 12-15.

Pantry Items
Dried lentils (1 1/2 cups)
Curry powder (2 tsp.)
Olive oil (1/2 cup)
Soy sauce (2 Tbsp.)
Ketchup (3/4 cup)
Fine seasoned bread crumbs (2 cups)
Cashews (1/3 cup, chopped)
Salt (1 tsp.)
Honey (1 Tbsp.)

Fresh Items
Onion (1)
Carrots (2)
Celery (2 stalks)
Garlic (3 cloves)
Green chili pepper (1)
Fresh basil (1 Tbsp., chopped)
Egg (1)
Plain yogurt (2 cups)
Fresh dill (2 Tbsp.)
Lemon juice (1 lemon)

KOFTAS
Dice onion, carrots, celery, 2 cloves garlic, basil, and chili pepper; in a large skillet, sauté in 1 tablespoon olive oil until tender. Add lentils to skillet and brown slightly. Mix soy sauce, curry, and ketchup with 2 1/2 cups water and pour over lentil mixture. Bring to boil. Cover and reduce heat. Simmer for 20 minutes until lentils are tender. Remove from heat. Add bread crumbs, cashews, and egg to cooled mixture. Shape into 1 1/2-inch balls. Drizzle with remaining oil. Bake in 350° F oven for 15 to 20 minutes.

YOGURT DIP
Mix 2 cups plain yogurt with 1 teaspoon salt; 2 tablespoons fresh dill weed, chopped; 1 garlic clove, minced; juice of one lemon; 1 tablespoon honey. Refrigerate 1 hour or overnight.

Inquisitions

The armed mob drags Jesus back to the high priest's palace in Jerusalem. First, He is presented to the household's patriarch priest, Annas. Annas is Caiaphas's father-in-law, and his age and position give him first crack at interrogating the prisoner while the rest of the Sanhedrin is hastily assembling in the main hall. Annas is eager to provoke the young Teacher into making a damaging statement. He has experience with this sort of thing. All they need is one good sound byte to undermine His credibility with the people and justify their actions. But Christ is not easily baited. "I have not conducted a secret conspiracy," He replies to Annas's questions. Christ's implied rebuke at this dead-of-night gathering hangs heavily in the air. "I have spoken openly." His three days of teaching in the temple courtyard have been an enormous thorn in the side of the duly appointed leaders. "The people know what I have said. Ask them." Annas takes His statement as a thinly veiled threat. A guard delivers a fierce blow across His face, almost sending Him to His knees. "Show more respect to a high priest," the guard bellows. "I spoke the truth," Jesus replies. "Why did you strike Me?" He will not be bullied into participating in their little charade of a trial. Christ declines to respond to the rest of Annas's insulting questions. They both know this is just the warm-up. Failing to provoke an incriminating statement from the Prisoner, Annas waves Him on in disgust. Jesus is escorted into the presence of Caiaphas, the high priest. What a difference a day can make! The renegade rabbi thronged with followers just a few days ago seemed invincible. He doesn't look so powerful now, standing with His hands tied behind His back in Caiaphas's grand hall. The assembled group is still groggy and a little wary. But they note with pleasure the welt forming across their adversary's cheek and the thin line of blood trickling down His jaw. The faces of the assembled Sanhedrin glisten with revenge and hatred. The inquisition begins. (See John 18.)

THOUGHT TO PONDER

❀ Do I sometimes give individuals in positions of authority more credibility than they are due?

"A book might be written on the injustice of the just."
—Anthony Hope, British writer, 1863-1933

THE LAST SUPPER
FAMILY ACTIVITY

Ages: Preschool to Adult
Materials Needed:
    Assorted candles
    Grape juice
    Passover food (see Middle Eastern recipes on Friday, Weeks 1, 2, 3, 4, and 11)

Suggested Readings:
Matthew 26:17-30; Mark 14:12-26; Luke 22:1-38; John 13; 14
The Desire of Ages by Ellen G. White, chapters 71-73
The Gift by Kim Johnson, chapters 2, 3
The Bible Story by Arthur S. Maxwell, vol. 9, part 2, stories 1-3 (for younger audiences)

Many Christian families enjoy commemorating Christ's Last Supper by celebrating a special dinner together. Plan a candlelight meal for your family or invite some friends to join you. Assign readings to various people, especially if the children present are old enough to read. Make sure to include a reading that even the littlest ones will enjoy. If the children are too young to sit through many readings, just pick one or two or continue one at bedtime. Appoint an individual to lead out. Light the candles. Turn off the lights. Enjoy the meal and the fellowship. Sing some hymns. Close the evening with a prayer circle. By tying the story of Christ to warm family memories, we bind our children to the gospel with the gentlest and strongest of ties. As the Lord has said, *"Do this in remembrance of me"* (Luke 22:19).

Traitors and Spies

When Peter is rebuked in the Garden of Gethsemane for resisting the armed mob, confusion and panic seize him. The pumping adrenalin that sent him eagerly into battle puts wings on his feet, and he flees into the darkness with the rest of the disciples. But Peter doesn't go far. He soon realizes that no one is chasing them. The lynch mob has gotten what they have come for, and they are no doubt headed back to Jerusalem with their captive. Peter knows their kind: rough men, eager for any excuse to use their fists. He cannot tolerate the thought of leaving the Master with them. He will at least follow. As Peter hastily makes his way back to the road, he almost bumps into John. Apparently they both have the same thought. Hurriedly they race along the dark paths until they catch sight of the torches in front of them. Slowing their pace, they dodge in and out of the shadows, carefully following the group to the front gate of the high priest's palace in Jerusalem. Considering the time of night, there seem to be a lot of people coming and going, but Peter isn't sure they can chance a frontal approach. The tall walls and iron gratings seem well designed to keep people in as well as out. John is young and less cautious.

Besides, he has been here before. The high priest is second cousin to his father's sister-in-law—or something like that.

The young girl at the gate looks familiar. John imagines that he can bluff his way in with a smile. It works. After checking out the lay of the land, he goes back to the gate for Peter. As it clangs shut behind them, Peter's heart sinks. Cautiously scanning the scene in front of him, he notices a familiar figure in the shadows of one of the upper rooms. Could it be Judas? Peter turns toward John. Their eyes meet as the sickening realization dawns. It is all becoming clear. Anger burns in Peter's throat. Judas has betrayed them all, and he and John have walked right into the trap! "Hey," the gate girl blurts out loudly, "Aren't you one of that Rabbi's disciples?" The soldiers by the fire glance over at Peter. John's eyes are wide with fear. "The hell, I am!" swears Peter as he spits into the fire. Suddenly there is a commotion on the stairs. The men in the courtyard momentarily forget Peter as they watch the prisoner dragged across the veranda. Judas turns toward the courtyard. Peter bows his head. (See Matthew 26; Mark 14; Luke 22; John 18.)

THOUGHTS TO PONDER

❀ Would I have been brave enough to follow Jesus into the camp of the enemy?

❀ Was Peter a brave man or a coward?

> *"Courage is not the absence of fear, but rather the judgment that something else is more important than fear."—Ambrose Redmoon*

PLANNING A FLOWER GARDEN

Planting a garden and watching it grow is an almost irresistible pleasure. Even if our "plot" is just a balcony or a tiny suburban lot, flowers can make a house a home. If you haven't done so already, grab a piece of graph paper and plan your flower garden now. Here's a checklist to help you organize your thoughts for a trip to the nursery to turn your dreams into reality.

Locations	Color Scheme	Flower Types	Supplies & Tools
Flower beds	Monochromatic Theme:	Shade loving	Potting soil
Containers	Shades of a single color	Sun loving	Fertilizer
Hanging plants	such as pink or yellow	Tall: 18+"	Ground cover
Window boxes	Coordinating Color Scheme:	Medium: 9"–16"	Mulch
Trellis	Complementary colors such as	Short: 2"–8"	Plastic liner
Raised beds	pastels, or red, white, and blue.	Cascading	Shovel
	Country Garden Mix:	Ground cover	Trowel
	A happy mix of many colors	Foliage	Hoe

Red Dawn

Caiaphas has put Jesus' trial together in great haste. Judas turned out to be more dependable than he had dared to hope. By sheer force as high priest, Caiaphas has assembled a scant quorum of the Sanhedrin, now seated red-eyed and yawning in his hall. Rounding up witnesses has been more problematic. It's so hard to get a credible witness on such short notice. The servants and ruffians he has hurriedly coached and bribed will have to do. He hopes his money has been well spent. Unfortunately, his players turn out to be more eager than skilled. They can't keep their stories straight. Such a simple task he's given them. Simple, simple lines, a child would be able to recite the lines; but, instead, they stumble wildly over their stories, contradicting one another.

Caiaphas scans the faces of the priests and learned scholars in front of him. Even his staunchest supporters are beginning to waver. The trial is too obviously a sham. What they are doing is politically risky. Perhaps it's too risky, they're thinking. He has to do something quickly, or all will be lost. Jesus has not denied any of the accusations. He hardly seems to be listening as if He is too proud to even

acknowledge these riffraff and their silly stories. Who does He think He is? That's it! Caiaphas springs to his feet. He waves away the confused witness and addresses Jesus directly. "Who do You think You are?" Christ still does not answer, but He is no longer staring at the floor. Caiaphas circles in for the kill. "May I remind You, You are under oath. I will ask You again. Who are You? Are You the Messiah? Are You the Son of God?" "I am," Jesus simply replies. The assembly gasps. Jesus has appropriated to Himself the title of God! And just in case anybody has been napping and has missed the point, He underscores it. "You will see Me, Caiaphas, when I descend from the heavens at the right hand of God." Caiaphas shrieks in mock piety and tears his robe. Down below, Peter, who has two more times denied that he is a disciple, stares up in disbelief. "What more do we need?" the high priest demands of the assembly. A rooster crows loudly above the din. Jesus turns toward the courtyard. "The blasphemer deserves death," the assembly roars back to Caiaphas. But Jesus is watching only Peter's face as the red dawn pours through the gates. (See Matthew 26; Mark 14; Luke 22; John 18.)

THOUGHTS TO PONDER

❀ Have I ever witnessed an angry group destroy the reputation of a good man or woman?
❀ Have I ever been afraid to stick up for someone who is disliked by the "right" people?

> *"A conscience without God is like a court without a judge."*
> *—Alphonse De Lamartine, French poet, 1790-1869*

FORGIVING A BETRAYAL

Have you ever experienced a serious betrayal? Even if you wish to forgive and move on, your anger and resentment may continue to disrupt your life. Remind yourself of these facts:

1. True reconciliation is a two-way street. There must be desire for forgiveness on one hand and granting of forgiveness on the other. If our betrayer does not acknowledge a need for forgiveness, we cannot experience true reconciliation. Christ was reconciled with Peter but not with Judas. Sometimes we are forced to grieve the loss of a relationship.
2. Before we are able to truly forgive, we must acknowledge that we have been hurt. If we feel it is weak to admit vulnerability, our pain festers, and we respond in unhealthy ways.
3. When we can honestly acknowledge our hurt and the one who has let us down acknowledges his or her failure, then true forgiveness and healing can begin.
4. Whether we are forced to grieve a broken relationship or to begin the hard job of rebuilding a damaged relationship, God will heal our broken hearts. The Great Healer can be trusted to restore our spirit and bring us peace if we ask Him.

Tale of Two Sinners

As dawn pierces the darkness and the rooster sings out his revelry, the full realization of what he has done breaks on Peter's heart. Jesus turns toward Peter. Standing centered and calm in the eye of the storm, Jesus is not broken. Peter knows that he will never again consider himself a brave man. He has behaved as a coward. While Jesus is still looking at him, a guard flings a cloak over Christ's head and hits Him with a stick. "Who hit You, Prophet?" the guard mocks. Peter can stand it no longer. He rushes out of the gate, running blindly down the narrow alleys as fast as he can, legs and lungs burning. When he can run no more, he collapses on the ground. He doesn't care who sees him. He has failed. He has utterly, completely failed Jesus. Every arrogant, bragging statement comes flooding back to his mind. Every foul vulgarity that he's used to deny Christ rings painfully in his ears. He covers his ears with his fists, unable to block out the sound of his own voice as sobs wrack his body.

Back at the temple palace, Judas watches in amazement as the Sanhedrin votes death to the young Rabbi. Judas hadn't thought it would come to this, but Jesus does not seem surprised.

He remains quiet and composed, even when surrounded by the murderous priests and angry mob. He looks like the Son of a God. The crowd responds to the death verdict with a sudden surge of violence, hitting, punching, and spitting on Christ. The priests make no effort to protect the prisoner. Blood starts seeping through His linen tunic. Judas is sickened by the scene in front of him. As they drag Jesus away, Judas rushes to the front of the hall. "He is innocent!" he screams at Caiaphas and the still-assembled Sanhedrin. They look on him with distain. For the first time, Judas can see himself in their eyes. He is horrified. "I have betrayed innocent blood," the truth is wrung out of his throat. It is too awful to contemplate. "What is that to us?" they reply cooly. "That's your responsibility." What an arrogant, hypocritical son of a . . . Judas angrily flings the bag of silver at Caiaphas, but the high priest ducks. The bag tears as it hits the wall, and the coins career wildly about the room. Judas rushes out of the room and through the same gate Peter has used just minutes earlier. One is broken; the other is destroyed. (See Matthew 26; 27; Mark 14; Luke 22; John 18; 19.)

THOUGHT TO PONDER

❦ Both Peter and Judas had strong points and shortcomings. What made the difference?

"To betray you must first belong."
—Harold Philby

THE LONG ROAD HOME

If you have ever failed someone miserably, you know how hard it is to regain that trust. When church members fail, sometimes we also find it hard to allow them back into the fold again. How should we treat church members who have experienced a public failure? How did Jesus treat Peter?

1. Jesus immediately accepted Peter's repentant heart.
2. Jesus did not punish, lecture, or scold Peter.
3. Jesus asked Peter to publicly declare his love and loyalty.
4. Jesus reaffirmed Peter's place among the disciples.
5. Jesus commissioned Peter with spiritual responsibilities.

Insomnia

In the palace of the governor, a woman standing on her balcony in the early morning light watches intently as a group of Jewish priests and local soldiers leads a bruised and beaten Prisoner up the path to the Praetorium. She hastily calls for her secretary. "Write a note to my husband," she commands. "He must have nothing to do with this Prisoner! Tell him I have suffered terrible dreams throughout the night on account of this Man."

A few blocks away Peter faces the morning a bitter and broken man. He has lived through his worst nightmare. Nothing he believed about himself at sunset the day before has survived the night. Why did he not stay awake with Christ in the Garden? Why did he sleep? Will his tortured mind ever find rest again?

Behind the prisoner a grief-stricken young man faithfully follows at a distance as his Master is escorted to the Roman governor. It has been a long and agonizing night. Yet John finds little comfort with the dawn.

The remaining disciples are scattered and hiding, anticipating at every sound the arrival of an armed guard with the morning light. They are too weary to run, too frightened now to sleep.

As the sun rises in the sky over Jerusalem, the lifeless body of Judas hangs just outside the city gates. His has not endured his nightmares. He has not survived the darkness. (See Matthew 27.)

THOUGHTS TO PONDER

❀ Why do our everyday fears seem larger and more frightening at night?

❀ How can I assure my children that Jesus is always near, even in the darkness?

"We are such stuff as dreams are made of, and our little life, is rounded with a sleep."
—William Shakespeare

NOW I LAY ME DOWN TO SLEEP

If you're like most people, you periodically experience difficulty sleeping. If your problem is persistent, long-term, or interfering with your ability to function, it is important to seek help from a doctor or a counselor. If your insomnia is occasional or the result of a specific crisis or unusual stress, you may find the following "Insomniac's Tool Box" helpful:

- ❀ **Avoid caffeine,** especially after noon. If you enjoy a hot drink before bedtime, try a relaxing herbal tea such as chamomile or peppermint.
- ❀ **Go to bed on time.** Don't stay up late to make yourself sleepy. It will only disrupt your sleep patterns further.
- ❀ **Maintain moderate exercise to drain off excess stress.** Even if lack of sleep is making you feel lethargic, keep up your exercise routine. If you haven't been exercising regularly, consider a walk after supper to help your body relax.
- ❀ **Make a list** of things you need to do tomorrow. You may find that once you commit what's nagging you to a "to do" list, that your mind relaxes and lets you doze off.
- ❀ **Don't panic when you awake** in the middle of the night. Relaxing is not as good as sleeping, but it can be regenerating. Relax by doing something you find enjoyable but not too stimulating, such as light reading, needlework, or crossword puzzles.
- ❀ **Occasional insomnia is not the end of the world.** Remind yourself that one or two restless nights will not seriously impair your energy level or ability to function.

Clean Hands

Pilate has just seated himself for breakfast when a servant announces that a contingent of the local clergy led by the high priest is outside demanding to see the governor. "Caiaphas himself at this hour?" Pilate inquires. "It must be important. Show them into the great hall." The servant hesitates. "Excuse me, Sir. It is the sixth day of Passover." "Of course it's the sixth day of Passover," Pilate snaps. "Who could miss the throng of pilgrims overrunning the city?" The servant still hesitates. "What is it, Man?" the governor demands. "They won't come in, Sir." The servant makes a slight nod toward Pilate's barely touched bacon and eggs. "If they enter your house, it will make them ceremonially unclean. They won't be able to eat the Passover supper tonight." Pilate throws his napkin down on the table. "Oh for heaven's sake!" he sputters. "What have I ever done to deserve this?" "One more thing, Sir." The servant is still hovering. "What now? Do I have to take a special bath or wave incense before I go out to see them?" The servant looks embarrassed. "Your wife has sent you a message." He holds out a note. "Put it by my breakfast. I hope to get to both shortly," Pilate instructs. "She said you were to read it before you saw the Prisoner." Pilate looks surprised. "Prisoner?" He takes the sheet of papyrus.

It's a dirty business dealing with these holy men, but someone's got to do it. It turns out to be dirtier than Pilate imagined. The holy men have shown up with an ill-tempered mob, dragging a young rabbi. Pilate can't get anyone to tell him what the problem is. The priests keep insisting the Man is the worst sort of troublemaker, worthy of death. The accused Man refuses to deny any of the charges. Finally they say the Man claims to be the Son of God, the King of the Jews. "He is a blasphemer deserving death!" His wife's note makes Pilate nervous about signing an execution order for the Son of God. He ushers the prisoner into his hall for a private chat. If one were to actually meet a god, how would one know for sure? In the end, Pilate cannot take the risk. The last thing he needs is a riot at Passover. The mob is screaming "Crucify Him!" What can he do? Pilate calls for a basin of water. He dramatically washes his hands. These holy men understand ceremonial cleansing. "His blood be on your hands," he pronounces. (See Matthew 27; Mark 15; Luke 22; 23; John 18; 19.)

THOUGHT TO PONDER

❀ Were the Jews in Christ's day unique as a religious group in that they put more emphasis on ceremony than integrity?

"As fall the dews on quenchless sands / Blood only serves to wash Ambition's hands!"
—Lord Byron

NO REGRETS

I've often heard celebrities comment that they have no regrets regarding their lives. Perhaps they mean they are willing to accept responsibility for both their good and bad choices, and I can respect that. But unlike most celebrities, I have dozens of regrets. Mostly I regret the uncharitable things I've said and the unkind things I've done. The rest of my choices I'm willing to live with. But there are words I wish I could take back and petty actions I wish I could undo. I challenge you to consider your regrets. Sit down with your journal or a sheet of paper and pen a "Regrets List." Examine what motivated you to do the things you regret most. Are there patterns you see emerging? Are there areas in your life in need of divine healing? Wouldn't it be wonderful if, as Christians, we could fellowship together with "no regrets"?

The Show Must Go On

That would be just like a bureaucrat! Herod blinks and rubs his eyes. It's too early to be interviewing malcontents. But obviously Pilate has been up for hours. They have a reputation for running a tight ship at the Praetorium. And with that pious wife of his, state dinners are notoriously sober affairs. Herodias, on the other hand, has a talent for parties. A servant hands Herod a goblet, and he gulps it down, hoping to quell the pounding in his head. "Whom did you say Pilate has sent to me, and what am I supposed to decide?" he asks again as his head begins to clear. "Jesus, the Prophet from Galilee. The priests say He has declared Himself King." Herod's eyes light up. "Jesus of Nazareth! Isn't He the One who does all the miracles? They say He can turn water into wine." Herod rubs his hands gleefully. "Finally a holy man I can appreciate! Oh, this is going to be fun." Herod splashes water over his face and runs his fingers through his hair. "Don't we have a few cripples about? Round them up. Let's see what kind of show this Healer can put on!"

Unfortunately, Jesus of Nazareth turns out to be rather a disappointment. Not that Herod was expecting much. He's heard these sorts of claims and stories before. In fact, he almost got sucked in by a wilderness mystic called John the Baptist, who spent some time as a guest in his palace dungeon not too long before. Of course, Herodias put an end to him. But the morning is not a total loss. The local clergy provide some comic relief. The Prophet has really gotten them stirred up. The holy men are so mad they can hardly spit their words out. It's quite amusing. Herod can't resist goading them on. He instructs the guards to costume the Prisoner as a king. Herod manages an unsteady bow with an extravagant flourish, "Your royal greatness, how can your humble servant, King Herod, be of assistance?" The soldiers erupt in wild laughter. Herod always had a dramatic flair. That's the problem with Judea, so little good theatre. "Send Him back to Pilate," Herod instructs when he finishes wiping the tears of laughter from his eyes. "And be sure to thank him for me. . . . No, no, no! Leave the costume on. Pilate will appreciate it." (See Luke 22.)

THOUGHT TO PONDER
❀ Have I ever considered how foolish religious disputes appear to the secular world?

COUSCOUS SALAD
MIDDLE EASTERN SALAD

This is a generous salad suitable for potlucks. Preparation time: 30 minutes. Serves 20+.

Pantry Items
Couscous or baby pastina (1 12-oz. box)
Raisins (1 cup)
Toasted almonds (1 cup, chopped)
Olive oil (1 cup)
Seasoned rice vinegar (1/4 cup)
Coriander (1/2 tsp.)
Cumin (1/2 tsp.)
Curry powder (1 tsp.)
Salt (1 tsp.)

Fresh Items
Onion (1 small)
Celery (2 stalks)
Lemon (1)

DIRECTIONS
Cook and drain couscous or baby pastina according to directions. Finely dice onion and thinly slice celery. Place in large mixing bowl. Add couscous, raisins, and almonds. Mix together gently. Squeeze the juice of one fresh lemon into small bowl (about 1/4 cup). Add coriander, cumin, curry powder, and salt to lemon juice and mix well. Add olive oil and rice vinegar to lemon juice and whisk briskly. Pour lemon-juice mixture slowly over couscous and gently toss to coat well. Cover and refrigerate 4 hours or overnight. Toss gently before serving.

Royal Robes

Attiring the prisoner in a regal cloak was a stroke of wicked brilliance. It transformed the condemned Man into a royal jester and allowed the boys to have some fun on an otherwise tedious work detail. While waiting for the cross to be assembled, they had some time to kill. The Prisoner had already been beaten twice—once in the temple palace and again at the Praetorium. The idea that He thought He was a king just struck them as funny and sparked their latent creative impulses. Someone fashioned a laurel of thorns for the "king." Someone else twisted reeds together to make a scepter. Gleefully mixing courtesies with crudeness, the macabre impromptu commenced. Christ, an effigy for all authority that had ever crushed them under heel, received the full force of their undigested hate. The soldiers aped a perverted, comedic court where the rulers, not the servants, were brutalized. As Christ allowed the robe of mortal authority to be placed on His bloody shoulders, the assembled universe watched in awe. A God was absorbing the force of blows and hatred earned by a thousand cruel despots. With each savage blow He allowed to fall on His omnipotently powerful being, He was weaving a robe of righteousness to fling upon the shoulders of ten thousand unworthy mortals. Was it ever a fair trade? What manner of love is this?

THOUGHT TO PONDER

❀ Could any of our good works ever compare to the robe of righteousness Christ has given us?

> "The Crucifixion and other historical precedents notwithstanding, many of us still believe that outstanding goodness is a kind of armor, that virtue, seen plain and bare, gives pause to criminality. But perhaps it is the other way around."
> —Mary McCarthy, American author, 1912-1989

PAPER FLOWER BASKETS
INSIDE ACTIVITY

Ages: Preschool to Grade School
Materials Needed:
    Tissue paper (1 package rainbow colors)
    Floral Styrofoam plastic foam blocks
    Pipe cleaners or floral wire
    Small baskets

This is a relatively low-expense project, but you will need to purchase the materials from a craft store ahead of time.

1. Unfold the tissue paper and lay flat on a table in one pile. (Do not separate the sheets.)
2. Cut the pile of tissue paper into large squares approximately 5 x 5 inches or larger. Sizes can vary.
3. Take one square pile of tissue paper and gently scrunch the two sides toward the middle to form a sort of bow-tie shape. Secure the center by twisting the floral wire or pipe cleaner around the middle. Twist the wire ends together to form the stem of the flower.
4. Now help your children carefully separate the sheets of tissue paper by gently pulling them one at a time up toward the center. The effect will look kind of like a rainbow-colored carnation.
5. Precut the Styrofoam blocks to fit the baskets. After the flowers are finished, help your children insert their flowers into the baskets by pushing the wire stems into the Styrofoam.
6. If desired, finish the basket by tying on a ribbon.

    These baskets make colorful gifts for friends, neighbors, shut-ins, or people in the hospital or a nursing home. Your children will enjoy giving their flower baskets as much as making them.

Stranger at the Gates

Who can say whether it was sheer force of will or divine strength? By the time they laid the cross on His shoulders, He had endured a nearly crushing encounter with unseen forces in the Garden of Gethsemane, a half dozen inquisitions with various priests and rulers, two public beatings that had no doubt left His back and shoulders shredded and raw, and a couple of free-for-alls, during which He had been tossed to the crowd for their brutal amusement. He had been spit upon, reviled, slapped, and mocked. A laurel of thorns had been pressed into His scalp. It was a wonder He was still standing when they laid the cross on His shoulders and ordered Him to march. It is no wonder that He didn't get far. "His form marred beyond human likeness" (Isaiah 52:14).

A stranger was pressed into service and forced to carry the cross He could not manage. We know the stranger's name, Simon of Cyrene. We know the names of his sons, Alexander and Rufus. Did they all become Christians? Were they members of the early apostolic church?

Perhaps Simon was led by God to be at the city gate as Christ's spent body finally collapsed. Perhaps he was just lucky. He may have been angry and resentful when the Roman soldiers pressed him into the revolting service of carrying a criminal's cross. But somehow I feel that he wasn't. I have a good feeling about Simon. I believe he felt compassion for the bruised and beaten Man beneath the cross. I don't know anything else about Simon of Cyrene. I don't know what accomplishments he had or whether he had any at all. But if the only purpose Simon had in life was to be the stranger at the gate when Christ needed him, I would think that would be worth being born for. Don't you wish it could have been you? What wouldn't you give to have been the one to provide a brief respite for Christ as He climbed the hill to Calvary? Was Simon foreordained by God for this honor, or was Simon of Cyrene just one of the luckiest men to ever walk the face of the earth? (See Matthew 27; Mark 15; Luke 23.)

THOUGHTS TO PONDER
❀ When I consider Christ's sacrifice for me, is there really any service too humble for me to perform?
❀ Am I willing to be used by Christ in any way He sees fit?

"Christianity demands a level of caring that transcends human inclinations."
—Erwin W. Lutzer, American minister

GARDEN GATES

If you've ever traveled in parts of the world in which garden gates are a thing of beauty, you know what it is to be enchanted. There is something about a garden path behind a lovely gate that beckons irresistibly. It says Welcome and bids guests to linger. Not all of us are lucky enough to live in a little cottage with a picket fence, but that doesn't mean we can't welcome our guests with a little garden enchantment. Following are some ideas guaranteed to make an entrance. This season why not select one or two or three garden touches that are right for your entry.

Hand-crafted gate	Hanging baskets
Trellis archway	Arrangement of flower pots
Rocking chairs	Window boxes
Garden bench	Welcome wreath
Porch swing	Climbing ivy or morning glory
Stone pathway	Dried-flower swag
Pretty welcome mat	Wall pots with flowers (pots flat on one side for mounting)

WEEK 5 — MONDAY

King of the Jews

Tychiucus took one look at the Prisoner and clenched his jaw. He'd obviously been worked over pretty well. Not much chance He'd make it up the hill. Stupid mistake! It's one thing to allow the boys to let off a little steam; it's another to let them beat the Prisoner to a pulp before He's dragged His cross up Golgotha. He had half a mind to order the moronic cretins to carry it themselves. The sergeant in charge instantly reads the disgusted look on the arriving centurion's face and quickly orders his men to remove the ridiculous costume and re-clothe the Prisoner. The Man's back is a raw slab of flayed flesh. When they lay the cross on His shoulders, the Prisoner staggers, but He doesn't collapse. Tychiucus has to hand it to Him. It isn't until they are outside the city gates that the Man's body finally gives out.

Tychiucus has been watching Him closely. It is a mystery why the condemned Man is exerting every last fiber in His beaten body to drag His own instrument of execution. An unlucky bystander is quickly pressed into service, but the fall has triggered a wild reaction from the women in the crowd. They send up a howl of sympathy for the fallen Prisoner, wailing and screaming as one would for the dead. Tychiucus quickly assesses the scene. This is the sort of thing that can spark a mob into violence. The Prisoner is dragged to His feet. As He rises, He turns His head toward the women. Tychiucus moves his hand to the hilt of his sword, his other hand ready to give the order. "Don't weep for Me, Daughters of Jerusalem," the condemned Man comforts them. The women quiet down. The procession moves forward. Tychiucus relaxes his grip. What manner of Man is this? When they arrive at the hill, Tychiucus removes a sealed scroll from his robe and hands it to the soldiers. Pilate has instructed that this scroll is to be tacked to the head of the cross. The inscription is written in three languages. "The King of the Jews" it reads. The Jewish leaders in the group are infuriated. They angrily demand that the inscription be changed to read, "He thinks he is the king of the Jews." Tychiucus glances over at the Prisoner. His face is bruised and swollen, but He is not snarling. His body is battered and bleeding, but He is not broken. Tychiucus is familiar with pain. He has never seen pain borne with such dignity. "Take up your complaints with Pilate," he gruffly orders the Jewish leaders as he turns his attention to the execution of their King. (See Luke 23.)

THOUGHT TO PONDER
❀ As Christians, are we sometimes guilty of becoming so intensely involved in doctrinal disagreements that we appear hopelessly out of touch to the secular world?

"A man who was completely innocent, offered himself as a sacrifice for the good of others, including his enemies, and became the ransom of the world. It was a perfect act."—Mahatma Gandhi

CIVIL DISOBEDIENCE

Today, as in Christ's day, governments are capable of brutality and tyranny. As Christians, where does our responsibility lie? When we observe injustice, how should we respond?

❀ Should Christians participate in nonviolent protests and movements?
❀ What about civil disobedience? Should Christians break the law to draw attention to injustice?
❀ Is it morally acceptable to break the law by harboring victims of political or religious persecution?
❀ Would it be wrong to support or fight in a revolution to overthrow a politically brutal regime?

In the 2,000 years since Christ lived on earth, Christians have walked a fine line between the kingdom of heaven and the kingdoms of this earth. Sometimes our allegiance between the two kingdoms has been in direct conflict. What would Christ do? How has Christianity failed in the past?

Lamb of God

Before the Roman soldiers nail their victim to the cross, they offer a curious comfort, wine mixed with a narcotic. Maybe it is easier to nail a drugged prisoner to a cross. But Christ is not resisting. He waves the numbing potion aside. This is not the bitter cup He has chosen to swallow. They bind His hands and legs to the wooden beams and pin His flesh to the cross, hoist it up, and drive it into the earth. "Father, forgive them," He pleads, "for they do not know what they are doing." The universe reels in shock. Below, demons and priests are euphoric. "Let God rescue Him now if He wants Him." They laugh in crazed delight at the sight of the naked Man, nailed to the cross, beaten beyond recognition. At His feet the bored soldiers roll dice for His tunic. Among the crowd Christ's mother gazes up at the disfigured body of her Son. She yearns to pull that battered face to her breast once more. In spite of His pain and anguish, He recognizes how unfair this is for her. Gently He entrusts her into the care of His disciple John, but her broken heart cannot be comforted.

God looks down from above. It is enough! Creation revolts. The sun refuses to shine. Darkness rolls across the landscape. The earth reels against the cruel cross impaling her surface. Hills and valleys seethe like the sea. The universe itself is pulling apart. The Creator is dying. In the city it is the ninth hour of a strange Passover. The lamb is prepared for the altar. As the priest's hand is raised, an archangel dispatched from the throne of God rends the veil that had shrouded the Most Holy Place from top to bottom. God is not there. The frightened priest drops his knife. The lamb escapes. On the hill the dying Man cries, *"Eloi, Eloi lama sabachthani?"* All eyes are on the center cross. "What did He say?" Heaven can take no more. "It is finished," the Son breathes, expelling His last breath into the darkness. The pagan centurion has read the portents and seen the omens in the sky. "Surely this is the Son of a god," he mutters. But all doubters have fled the hill. (See Luke 23.)

THOUGHTS TO PONDER
- How must Mary have felt, gazing upon the brutalized body of her Son, unable to protect Him?
- Did Mary understand that crucifixion was what Jesus was born for?

"A mother who is really a mother is never free."—Honore De Balzac

THE HAND THAT ROCKS THE CRADLE

Mothers have the first, and many believe the most formative, influence on a child. At some point, we step back to allow our children to develop other relationships. As they mature into adulthood, we hope that their relationship with Christ becomes the most formative influence in their lives. But it doesn't happen automatically. Consider ways that you can encourage your children to develop a strong personal relationship with God:

❀ Pray with your children on a daily basis. Start young and continue to pray with them through their teen years. Allow your children to see you talking to God as a friend.

❀ Even if it's only ten or fifteen minutes a day, set aside daily devotional time with your children. As they grow, encourage them to select the devotional readings. Pursue their spiritual interests. Talk about the things that come naturally. Wrap warm memories around worship time.

❀ Stay spiritually open. Sometimes we feel awkward discussing religious things. But our children don't have to feel awkward if we make a point to keep spiritual viewpoints a part of our daily communication. It is not necessary to force the issue. Just ask their opinion and listen. Children are remarkably open to discussions about God. Cherish and encourage their interest.

Seal the Tomb

When he washed his hands in front of the mob, Pilate thought he made it clear that he was done with them. But the priests refused to give him peace. It wasn't long before they were back, as angry as before. They didn't like the inscription he had penned for the Prisoner's cross and were demanding that he change it. "What I have written I have written," he snapped angrily. They could push him only so far. But by mid-afternoon, they were back again. This time they wanted Pilate to instruct the soldiers to break the crucified convict's legs and haul the convicts down before sunset so they wouldn't hang over the city during the high Sabbath. The priests should have thought of that earlier, but he granted their request. No need to stir up the crowds.

Then the weather took an awful turn. A storm that refused to rain thundered and flashed in an eerie darkness for almost three hours. Earthquakes shook and rumbled through the city. Pilate's wife took it as a bad omen. She was in near hysteria. It made Pilate a little edgy too. No sooner had the storm passed, when yet another contingent arrived, requesting the body of Jesus. Certainly the Man wasn't dead already? Two wealthy Jewish scholars insisted that He was indeed dead. Was this a trick? Pilate called for the centurion on duty. The hardened veteran nodded grimly. The Prisoner called the King of the Jews was dead. They had pierced His side with a spear to make sure. Blood and water flowed; there was no doubt. Pilate signed over the body. But he couldn't shake an uneasy feeling. His wife's superstitions, along with this nasty business, were starting to unnerve him. By dawn the priests were back on his doorstep. "Isn't this supposed to be your day of rest?" he grumbled, "What now?" The priests said the Man had claimed that He would rise from the dead on the third day. Pilate's blood ran cold. He gazed intently at the faces in front of him. They tried to cover their apprehension with the excuse that the Man's disciples might steal the body and start rumors, but their eyes betrayed them. They were afraid. He sent soldiers with them. "Make the tomb as secure as you know how," was the order from the governor. How do you secure a dead man? The centurion posted his troops and set the Roman seal over the opening. What else did they want him to do? (See Matthew 27; Luke 23; John 19.)

THOUGHTS TO PONDER
❀ Have I ever compromised with what I knew was right?
❀ Did I find, as Pilate did, that it became impossible to stop with just one concession?

"An appeaser is one who feeds a crocodile, hoping it will eat him last."—Winston Churchill

COMPROMISES

There are two types of compromise. The one compromise is with our selfishness, the necessity to consider other's wants and needs. The other compromise is with our integrity, when we feel the pressure to bend our principles. One is admirable; the other is dangerous. How do we tell the difference? How do we develop one and deny the other? When we are feeling pressure to compromise, we can pass our compromises through a quick litmus test:

1. Will a compromise violate any moral or ethical standards? If the answer is No, strive for a compromise. Set your preconceived ideas aside and work for an equitable solution.
2. Will a compromise diminish you or another person in some way? If the answer is Yes, stand your ground. It is not selfish to refuse a compromise that will impair your effectiveness, your health, your mental well-being, or your calling.
3. Will a compromise breach your integrity? If the answer is Yes, no matter how minor the compromise seems, it is not worth it. Even a small compromise can have a hefty price tag.

He Is Not There

When the Creator, the great I Am, the Prince of Peace, awakens from death and emerges from the tomb, the universe erupts. Death is conquered, evil is dealt a lethal blow, a bridge is forged between the land of darkness and the courts of heaven. Christ has thrown His body across the abyss. We have a passage to safety. But mortal men see only the lightning and the earthquake. And that is frightening enough. The guards desert their post in terror. Some run like evil minions to their masters, the priests, and concoct a lie for a pretty price. Some spread the word in the streets. Confusion reigns. Perhaps it was just lightning and earthquakes. Jerusalem has experienced some nasty storms in the past few days. But it is not the end of the world, is it?

On the way to the tomb, Mary Magdalene and the rest of the women feel the earthquakes and see the lightning, but the gaping tomb is still a surprise. He is not there! It is too much. First His horrible death, now this! Mary runs back to where Peter and John are hiding. "They have taken Him. He is not there!" She is almost incoherent with grief. The two men race to the tomb, with Mary following on their heels. John gets there first. The heavy covering has been pushed aside. He peers in. He hesitates to enter. He can see the winding linen unraveled on the floor. The ghastliness of the scene seizes him. He has seen so much; he does not doubt the enemy is capable of any depravity. Peter rushes past him into the bowel of the tomb itself. Peter finds the shroud folded neatly on the stone slab. He stands dumbly trying to put the pieces together into some scenario that makes sense. Nothing makes sense. He is not there.

Mary stands outside weeping. "Woman, why are you weeping?" the gardener asks. "They have taken my Lord away. Please tell me where they have put Him," she begs. She does not care what they have done to His body. She will tend to it. She will not be denied this last ministry of love. "Tell me where you have put Him and I will get Him," she pleads. "Mary," the Lord of heaven and earth gently calls her name. (See Matthew 28; Mark 16; Luke 24; John 20.)

THOUGHTS TO PONDER
- Have I ever been surprised by the goodness of God?
- Have I ever doubted that God's goodness and blessings were meant for me?

"The Lord has turned all our sunsets into sunrises."—Clement of Alexandria, A.D. 150-220

LEANING INTO MIRACLES

The resurrected God can breathe life into our lives as well. Not just at the Second Coming but now, today. Broken dreams, broken relationships, and broken spirits revive under His holy breath. We usually try so hard to offer God our best. Instead, try offering Him your worst: your heartaches and failures, your weaknesses and bad habits, your disappointments and failures. It's not a trick. It's not a con. God will turn your dross into gold, your weeping into joy. He will bless you with the desires of your heart because He can read your heart. You don't have to be worthy. You only have to desire to be the woman that God created you to be. I challenge you today to turn your life over to the one Person in the universe whom you can really trust. Lean into the miracle of His love. He will not let you down. Open your life to His changes, and He will change your life. "Jesus promised His disciples three things: that they would be entirely fearless, absurdly happy, and in constant trouble," says W. Russell Maltby. Can you live with that?

Peace Be With You

Peace is so elusive for mortal men and women. Even while He should have been preparing for His encounter with evil in Gethsemane, Christ labored to bring peace to His disciples' troubled hearts. They never grasped that the battle for redemption was His alone to fight. They railed against the inevitable and struggled to change what must transpire. Their stupidity, cowardice, and denials would loom like mountains in their minds when in reality the only actions of any consequence were Christ's alone. To ask them to trust Him was faith of monumental proportion. He would not love them less for failing. And when it was finished, He would gently move them past their failures into joy because He had not failed.

On Sunday evening following Passover, the disciples gather in a closed room. There is no peace, only fear, confusion, and regret, when into the darkness walks the Prince of Light. "Peace be unto you," He greets them. "Why are you troubled? It is I, Myself. Touch Me." They have been through a terrible shock, but now they are filled with joy. Now they are ready to trust Him. Now they will listen. During the next forty days, He leads them through the plan of salvation from Genesis to Isaiah. "Peace be with you." He presses Thomas's hands into His scarred side. "Stop doubting and believe." Thomas drops to his knees. "My Lord and my God!" He singles out Peter. "Do you love Me, Peter?" He asks in front of the group. "You know I do, Lord," Peter replies. He knows. "Feed My sheep, Peter," He commands so everyone can hear. There is no lingering doubt, no repressed shame, and no hidden failures—for all have failed miserably. There is only one question, "Do you love Me? If you love Me, love one another. Do you love Me? If you love Me, care for My sheep. Do you love Me? If you love Me, you will have peace because no matter what happens, I will keep you safe for eternity." (See Luke 24 and John 21; 22.)

THOUGHTS TO PONDER

❀ Is love the most important part of the Christian walk?

❀ Can living a good life compensate for not having a relationship with Christ?

"Evangelism is the spontaneous overflow of a glad and free heart in Jesus Christ."
—*Robert Munger*

FRESH MUSTARD RICE BAKE
SEASONAL PRODUCE

This casserole uses one of the earliest garden greens, mustard greens. If you can get it fresh—great! If it's from your own garden, so much the better! Preparation time: 20 minutes. Baking time: 40 minutes. Serves 6–8.

Pantry Items
Rice (2 cups)
Olive oil (1/4 cup)
Soy sauce (3 Tbsp.)
Pine nuts (1/2 cup)

Fresh Items
Fresh mustard greens (4 cups, shredded)
Onion (1)
Garlic (3 cloves)
Fresh grated Parmesan cheese (1 cup)

DIRECTIONS
Dice onion and mince garlic. Heat oil over low heat in medium fry pan. Sauté onion, garlic, and pine nuts until onion is tender and translucent. Rinse mustard greens well, drain and shred. Add to pan and toss gently until slightly wilted. Remove from heat. In a 2-quart casserole dish with lid combine rice, soy sauce, cheese, and 4 cups of water. Mix well. Fold in greens. Cover with lid. Casserole may be refrigerated overnight. Bring to room temperature and mix gently before baking at 350° F for 25 minutes, remove lid. Bake an additional 15 minutes or until center bubbles.

Witnesses

Now it is time to leave them. He has spent three years with this small group. They have witnessed what it is for God to walk with men. They have witnessed miracles of incredible power as He has calmed the storms, raised the dead, faced down demons, and fed 5,000 men with nothing more than a little boy's lunch. They have experienced His tender ministry as He has preached on the hillsides, held the children in His arms, washed their dirty feet, and prepared them breakfast on the beach. They have witnessed a God who does not consider it beneath Him to be counted as one of us. The have witnessed Calvary. They have seen the extent to which God will go to redeem men and women from darkness.

They have also experienced what it is to fail the Living God. They have experienced the anguish of remorse and the depth of His forgiveness. They know what it is to be reconciled to God. They have no more illusions of integrity or bravery. They know beyond all shadow of a doubt that they are weak and selfish, full of pride, and totally unworthy of His attention, let alone His love. Yet that He loves them completely is the one thing they are most sure of. They have been broken and emptied. They are finally ready to be filled. It is time for Him to return to the Father. Their hour has come. As the angels lift Him into the heavens, they watch with tears streaming down their faces and His words ringing in their ears. "You will receive power when the Holy Spirit comes on you; and you will be my witnesses in Jerusalem, and in all Judea and Samaria, and to the ends of the earth." "Surely I am with you always, to the very end of the age" (Acts 1:8 and Matthew 28:20).

THOUGHTS TO PONDER

❀ Am I ready to be broken and emptied and loved by God?

❀ Am I ready to be a "witness"?

> *"The men who followed Him were unique in their generation. They turned the world upside down because their hearts had been turned right side up. The world has never been the same."*—Billy Graham

STATE PARK VISIT
OUTSIDE ACTIVITY

Ages: 5 to Adult
Materials Needed:
    Water bottles for each member
    Trail mix or snacks
    Comfortable hiking shoes and socks
    Hats or caps
    First-aid pack
    Binoculars
    Field guide for birds or wildflowers

Summer is a great time to visit a park or recreation area. In the summer the parks abound with wildflowers, birds, and wildlife of every type, even butterflies. Plan a Sabbath expedition to enjoy God's wonderful creation. Pick trails that the entire family can manage safely and enjoy. Free trail maps and advice are usually available at the park center. Take along field guides on birds or wildflowers, and try to identify as many species as you can on your hike. Be sure to take along some water and light snacks for the walk. Remember to pack out whatever you bring in.

Before You Were Formed

Before you were formed in your mother's womb, before you were less than a speck, less than the tiniest pin prick of light, God conceived of you in His mind. As you were woven together in your mother's womb, with delicate strands of DNA spinning to create the woman you would become, He saw the whole of you. He dreamed the tiny infant, the beautiful baby, the curious toddler, the wide-eyed school girl, the confused teenager, and the emerging woman. He saw you become the daughter of God. His dream does not end. It arcs across eternity like a celestial rainbow. He dreams the role only you can play, the beauty and radiance only you will impart to His grand creation. He dreams of things more wonderful for you than your parents could ever imagine as they held you for the first time in their arms, believing all things possible began with you. They do.

On a dark planet with only a dim shadow of the eternal reality to be glimpsed, He carefully guides you toward your destiny. He will not lose you. There is no place you can go that He cannot find you. He will pursue you to the ends of the earth. He will rescue you from uncertainty and fear and failure. He will sustain you through loss and illness and aging. He will carry you safely across that dark river and set you on the shores of eternity. Before you were formed, God conceived of you in His mind.

THOUGHTS TO PONDER

❀ How can the knowledge that God has a special role for me, not only now but forever, impact my day-to-day life?

❀ As I watch my beautiful children grow and develop, does it give me a glimpse of how God sees me?

"Everyone has inside of him a piece of good news. The good news is that you don't know how great you can be! How much you can love! What you can accomplish! And what your potential is!"—Anne Frank

THE LITTLE FOXES

Every garden attracts a certain number of uninvited guests, be it damaging insects, sneaky bunnies, or fly-by birds. If you hate spraying chemical pesticides but also resent sharing the fruits of your labor with nature's little freeloaders, consider some "natural" remedies that old farmers swear by. Disclaimer: All natural remedies are better at discouraging than totally preventing garden pests. In God's economy, gleaners are part of the ecosystem.

Scarecrows. The most effective scarecrows flap in the breeze and make noise when they blow. They work for early spring seeds before the birds get savvy to the harmless scare.

Marigolds. Some gardeners swear by marigolds as a natural pesticide. Plant these colorful flowers between rows of vegetables. They do seem to discourage some caterpillars.

Mothballs. Some farmers sprinkle mothballs around their vegetables to ward off rabbits, but mothballs are poison to humans and cannot be used in a garden to which young children have access.

Beer bath. Plant-damaging slugs are attracted to the yeast in beer and are drawn to shallow bowls of beer, where they drown.

Flypaper. Good old-fashioned sticky paper attracts and traps insects.

Ladybugs. These little beetles can be purchased from garden nurseries to reduce the aphid population.

Early Memories

What is your earliest memory? What is the first image you can remember? Scientists say that we cannot remember much before five years of age, but I bet you have a few special images that predate kindergarten. I have a distinct memory of my father tickling my stomach on a diaper changer in the kitchen when he came home from work one evening. The memory is extraordinarily vivid. I see my father walking through the kitchen door. I know that it is evening after the sun has set. I see the smile on his face when he sees me. I see my mother moving to one side as he reaches down to tickle me. I have always cherished this as my first memory, a happy bonding moment between my parents and me.

As I grew older, it occurred to me that a diaper changer would probably not be in a kitchen. That more than likely the diaper changer was in the bedroom. I accepted that my memory was a fond fiction—not an actual event. I was surprised to learn some years later that my parents did indeed place a diaper changer inside the back door of their home to facilitate the busy comings and goings of a young preacher's family. Have you ever wondered what your child's first memory is? We never know when we are going to create that moment, do we? For a few short years, we are the guardians of the sons and daughters of God. What an awesome responsibility. What a magnificent honor. Love them well!

THOUGHTS TO PONDER
- What sort of memories am I developing for my children?
- Do my earliest memories impact my life in positive or negative ways?

"You are told a lot about your education, but some beautiful, sacred memory, preserved since childhood, is perhaps the best education of all. If a man carries many such memories into life with him, he is saved for the rest of his days. And even if only one good memory is left in our hearts, it may also be the instrument of our salvation one day."—Fyodor Dostoevski

THE STUFF OF MEMORIES

Memories are connected not only to events but also to sounds, emotions, sensory touch, and smell. You can use sensory triggers to wrap your children in memories that will sustain them through difficult times, long after you are no longer there to comfort them. Consider some of your own sensory triggers. Is it the smell of fresh pine needles at Christmas, a cuddle while reading together, the stroke of your hair, a special meal? Following are a few sensory triggers that you can cultivate and develop to communicate your love without a word.

- ❀ **The sense of smell.** Smell is an especially strong sensory trigger. If your children associate specific smells with happy memories, that scent will forever trigger warmth and comfort for them.
- ❀ **The sense of touch.** How do you touch your children when they make you especially happy? Do you pat their heads, stroke their cheeks, rub their shoulders? That special touch can bridge the communication gap during difficult times. Use it wisely.
- ❀ **The sense of taste.** Do your children have special meals that only you can make the way they like? Even after separation and conflict, that meal can open up doors of trust and intimacy.
- ❀ **The sense of sound.** Are happy times wrapped in the sounds of special songs or instruments for your children? Chances are that for the rest of their lives, safety and comfort will be associated with those sounds.

Playing Dress-Up

Playing dress-up is a perennial favorite of children. When we were young, we loved to feel grown-up, important, interesting. It didn't matter whether it was a tiara or a helmet that we pulled on—the headgear changed the way we felt about ourselves. Playing dress-up gave us an illusion of power and importance. We no longer felt small.

Big girls still like to play dress-up, don't we? We are suckers for TV and magazine makeovers. We love comparing "before" and "after" photos of ugly ducklings transformed into beautiful swans. We probably have lucky shoes, a favorite suit, or a special evening dress that we would wear every day if we could get away with it. When we slip into those garments, we step into a heightened sense of ourselves. We feel as if we are more than we were before. We feel stronger, sexier, and smarter. We may find that other people even treat us differently. It's all based on an illusion. Underneath we are still the same. But someday that will change too. In a moment, in a twinkling of an eye, we will be changed from mortality into immortality. We will shed our imperfect bodies for glory. We will be clothed in the glowing robe of His righteousness, and we will surround the throne of God as daughters in the courts of the King. Someday our Prince will come.

THOUGHTS TO PONDER

❀ In spite of my imperfect life and body, can I still believe that I am beautiful in God's eyes?

❀ Does understanding that I am a daughter of God affect my life in important ways?

"Fashion is the science of appearance, and it inspires one with the desire to seem rather than to be."—Henry Fielding, British novelist, 1707-1754

A WORKING WARDROBE

As a career consultant, I was often asked by women reentering the job market about building a professional wardrobe. There are image consultants, professional buyers, and personal coaches who do an excellent job grooming women for success. If you are entering a management or executive position, you may find that employing the services of such a professional is well worth the investment. If hiring a personal image consultant is not an option at the moment, the following suggestions are tried-and-true guides that can help you project a professional image without breaking the bank:

❀ Take the advice of the French and purchase the best little black skirt you can afford. A plain, lined black skirt of durable material such as light-weight wool gabardine can be worn two to three times a week with different outfits and will always look great.

❀ A well-constructed blazer worn over just about anything will project a professional image. Start with one or two blazers in neutral colors and add seasonal blazers as needed. Make sure your blazers fit well buttoned or unbuttoned, that the sleeves are not too long or too short, and that the lapels don't curl up as the day progresses.

❀ Select black leather for business accessories such as briefcase, portfolio, handbag, wallet, and shoes. Black is the easiest color to coordinate and will keep you looking pulled together. Brown, navy, burgundy, and tan are also great business colors but are more difficult and costly to coordinate.

❀ Maintain your wardrobe. Pick one evening a week to check your business wardrobe for needed repairs. Torn hems, missing buttons, scuffed shoes, and scratched handbags can seriously impair a professional image.

The Mommy Myth

There is a certain myth I call "The Mommy Myth" that assumes that when a woman becomes a mother she will intuitively know how to care for her baby. Nothing could be farther from the truth. I believe that when a tiny infant is placed in a new mother's arms, a miracle of love and bonding takes place. But I don't believe love automatically translates into useable data for caring for the infant. Today, with families flung from one end of the country to the other, many new mothers return from the hospital alone with their precious infant and hardly a clue about what to do next. In spite of an avalanche of books and magazines on parenting, many young mothers are overwhelmed. Should I nurse or bottle-feed my infant? Are disposal diapers or cloth diapers better for the baby? Should I feed the baby when it cries, or should I keep it on a strict schedule? Is it safe to leave the baby alone in its crib, or would it be better to keep it in my bed? Why won't my baby stop crying? Is that normal or is there something wrong with it? The list of questions is endless.

Advice is usually contradictory. What can a young mother do? It doesn't matter how intelligent, accomplished, or competent you are. Becoming a new mother is guaranteed to make you feel stupid. That's "The Mommy Truth." Luckily, infants are surprisingly resilient and will survive nursing or formulas, disposable or cloth diapers, and scheduled or unscheduled feedings. Apparently the one thing an infant can't survive is lack of love. No matter how well an infant is physically cared for, if it is not held and cuddled, it does not thrive. If you have questions about your new baby, don't be shy about asking your doctor, mid-wife, nurse, or social worker. There really aren't any stupid questions when it comes to the care of your baby. Just remember, the most important thing you can do is to love and enjoy your infant. This is the beginning of a beautiful friendship!

THOUGHTS TO PONDER
* Do I take time to really enjoy my children?
* Do I believe my mother enjoyed her children? How has that impacted my life?

"Except that right side up is best, there is not much to learn about holding a baby. There are one hundred and fifty-two distinctly different ways—and all are right! At least all will do."
— Heywood Broun, American journalist, 1888-1939

CRY-BABIES

All babies cry. Having a baby that cries a lot doesn't mean you're a bad mother any more than having a baby that rarely cries means you're a good mother. Each baby is different when it comes to crying. The best advice is to consult your pediatrician if you are concerned about the amount of crying your baby is doing. Other than that, it is helpful to bear the following in mind:

❇ If your baby cries a lot, it is referred to as a "colicky" baby; but that does not necessarily mean that it is experiencing stomach pains. No one is really sure why some babies cry excessively. Some pediatricians believe that some infants have not yet learned to relax and go to sleep naturally and become overly stimulated, unable to let down.

❇ Some calming techniques that *may* help: wrapping baby snuggly in a receiving blanket, giving a pacifier, patting on the back, pressing a cuddly toy against their tummies.

❇ Even extremely colicky babies usually outgrow it by the fourth or fifth month. Because a baby is colicky does not mean that it will be a difficult child.

❇ Constant crying can shred a parent's nerves. If you feel yourself reaching a breaking point, lay the baby in the crib and leave the room for ten minutes or so until you can regain your sense of calm.

Children of Adoption

We are fascinated by stories of adoption. In the first book of the Bible, we read about Moses, the son of a slave, adopted by a princess to become a prince of Egypt. The orphaned Esther is adopted by Mordecai and becomes the queen of Persia. In the movie *Ben-Hur,* a Jewish slave is adopted into the family of a Roman nobleman and becomes the renowned Ben-Hur. The birth of a child into a family is a wonderful thing, but an adoption is something special. An adopted child has been chosen. There are no questions regarding the intentions of an adopted parent. There has been no mistake, no happenstance, no accident. Adopted children know beyond a shadow of a doubt that their parents eagerly desired to love them and make them a part of their family. Under ancient Roman law, natural-born children could be disowned by their families— but never adopted children.

Perhaps that is why in the first century, Paul found the legal process of adoption a perfect analogy for God's grace. Although we were born slaves to corruption on a sinful planet, through Christ we have been redeemed and adopted as sons and daughters of God. As the apostle Paul says, we can now call God "Abba, Father!" We are heirs to the kingdom of heaven. Can we even comprehend the implications of that reality? What amazing grace!

THOUGHTS TO PONDER
- Have I ever considered what an honor it is to be an adopted child?
- Have I ever considered adopting a child?

"The best inheritance a parent can give his children is a few minutes of his time each day."
—*Orlando A. Battista*

ADOPTION

Adoption is an amazing journey of love. But, unfortunately, it can also be a long journey filled with heartache and disappointments. Adoption requires careful thought, diligent planning, and a firm commitment. If you are prayerfully considering adoption, the following Web sites can help provide you with solid information regarding your options, rights, and responsibilities:

❀ <www.ncfa-usa.org> is sponsored by the nonprofit organization, the National Council For Adoption. It is a particularly well-designed site, allowing the user to easily access information. It includes information regarding adoption agencies, attorneys, current legislation, research studies, and general information and guidelines regarding adoption.

❀ <www.calib.com/naic> is sponsored by the US Department of Health and Human Services. It links information from four government agencies regarding adoption information and opportunities. It is a comprehensive resource providing information on all aspects of the adoption process.

❀ <www.adventistadoption.com> is sponsored by the nonprofit organization Adventist Adoption and Family Services. It is committed to assisting Adventist families and birth parents with adoption services. Both domestic and international adoption opportunities are available through this service.

Mothers of the Church

Any church that is not blessed with a "church mother" is a poor church indeed. You know what I'm talking about. A church mother is the personification of unconditional acceptance. It doesn't matter whether you're up or down or having a bad-hair day, the church mother is always delighted to see you. When you talk to her, you have her complete attention. When you confide in a church mother, your secrets will never come back to haunt you. A church mother always encourages you and never loses faith in you. A church mother always sees the diamond in the rough and knows that God has great plans in store for you. She is always willing to spend a few moments in prayer with you. I've known several wonderful church mothers. Some have seen their children grow and move away. But few church mothers actually have children of their own. They are always surprised when they receive the most carnations on Mother's Day Sabbath. "But I'm not a mother," they say, a little embarrassed by the tokens of motherhood they are holding in their arms. Yes, you are! Thank God you are. We need you, and we are so grateful to have you. Once a year is not too often to say, "We recognize who you are. You are a church mother! Thank you."

THOUGHTS TO PONDER

❀ Does my church recognize and appreciate the church mothers in the congregation?

❀ Is there a special church mother I can honor this year who may not have children in the area?

"What do girls do who haven't any mothers to help them through their troubles?"
—*Louisa May Alcott*

OLIVIER POTATO SALAD
PICNIC OR POTLUCK

This delicious Russian-style potato salad carries well to a picnic or a potluck. Preparation time: 25 minutes. Serves 6-8.

Pantry Items
Salt (1 Tbsp. + 1 tsp. or to taste)
Mayonnaise (1 cup)

Fresh Items
New potatoes
  (8 cups, chopped)
Onion (1)
Carrots (2)
Frozen peas (1 cup)
Boiled eggs (2)
Sour cream (1/2 cup)
Dill (1 Tbsp. fresh or 1 tsp. dried)

DIRECTIONS
Bring large pot of water with 1 tablespoon of salt to boil. Add scrubbed and chopped new potatoes (you can leave the skins on) to the boiling water. Reduce heat and simmer. Meanwhile, cut onion into 8 wedges and slice carrots into 1/4 -inch rounds. After potatoes have boiled for 10 minutes, add onions and carrots to simmering potatoes. Allow to simmer for 5 more minutes or until potatoes are fork tender. Drain and rinse vegetables in cold water. While vegetables are draining, mix mayonnaise, sour cream, dill, and 1 teaspoon salt in a large mixing bowl. Chop boiled eggs and mix into mayonnaise. Add thoroughly drained vegetables and frozen peas to mixing bowl. Fold together gently but thoroughly. Add salt and/or pepper to taste. Refrigerate 4 hours or overnight.

Just a Twinkle

Starting with a smile and a tender glance, a new life is ushered into eternity by an act of love. How fitting. What a miscarriage of God's intent for births begun any other way. Violence and cruelty sometimes mar the inception of the greatest miracle, yet we are all washed in the same cleansing blood. Emerging from the womb, we are claimed by Christ. He is the great Life-Giver, the Creator, the Breath of Life. We belong to Him. Every child is a child of God. His plan for us transcends time and space. We are—because He desires us to be. Our legitimacy is authorized in the courts of heaven by decree of a child born in a stable without a paternal heritage. We are children of an Almighty God. Earthly parents are wise or foolish—sometimes even cruel—but our earthly origins are not our destiny. We have all been predestined for glory. During this short voyage, we must love the children well. We must recognize their divine destiny. We must guide them tenderly toward the heavenly Father. The safety of all children is our responsibility.

"Whoever welcomes a little child like this in my name welcomes me. But if anyone causes one of these little ones who believe in me to sin, it would be better for him to have a large millstone hung around his neck and to be drowned in the depths of the sea" (Matthew 18:5, 6).

THOUGHT TO PONDER

❀ Am I prepared to love, nurture, and protect all children in my life, whether they are my biological children or not?

"High birth is an accident, not a virtue."—Pietro Metastasio, Italian poet, 1698-1782

NATURE MONO-PRINT
OUTSIDE ACTIVITY

Ages: 8 to Adult
Materials Needed:
>   A canvas bag or bucket for collecting
>   Liquid acrylic paint, stencil paint, or thick poster paint
>   Large pieces of stiff paper (such as construction paper, heavy art paper,
>   or poster board)
>   Stiff brush or stencil brush
>   Newspaper

The object is to create a "one-of-a-kind print" using objects found on a nature hike. Collect objects that will make an interesting imprint, such as leaves, feathers, shells, ferns, or wildflowers. Spread newspapers on the table. Use the brush to gently stipple the paint onto the object. (Apply paint in an up-and-down motion instead of traditional brush strokes to prevent damaging fragile leaves and feathers.) Place the object, paint side down, on the paper. If necessary, cover object with a layer of newspapers and press down on it to make a clear imprint. Peel newspaper back carefully to avoid moving the object. Carefully lift the object. Repeat with another object until your entire collection is imprinted or a design you like emerges. Try using objects repeatedly to make interesting patterns. After the paint dries, date and sign your unique "mono print." It will be a wonderful souvenir of a beautiful day. You may even want to mount it or frame it.

Great Expectations

"You're going to have a baby!" Do you remember that moment of discovery? I'm sure you do. I had been married for only two months, and a baby definitely wasn't on our agenda. After feeling as if I had the flu for a week and a half and never actually developing a fever, I decided to visit the local drugstore for a pregnancy test. I was apprehensive and worried. I told nobody about the pregnancy test, not even my husband. Suddenly there it was—a clear, undeniable positive result. We were going to have a baby! I could not have anticipated in a hundred years the explosion of joy that rocked my body. Wasn't I supposed to be nervous, disappointed, afraid? Not that first day. All I could think of was that right now, at this moment, the tiniest little person was forming inside of me. What an incredible miracle! My husband was understandably shocked when I awoke him with the joyous news. But my excitement was unquenchable. It was like an avalanche overwhelming all doubts.

Some women are very discreet about early pregnancy for a lot of wise reasons. But I was not wise. I was ecstatic. I tried to act as if it were just another Sabbath morning, but I couldn't resist whispering our little secret to my best friend, who whispered it to her boyfriend, who mentioned it to a coworker. By the end of church, half the congregation was smiling back at us. Great expectations! What joy, what anticipation. Does God in heaven really look down upon us like an expectant mother, as Paul suggests? I bet He does. Someday we will emerge from this dark world as from a womb, and we will see God face-to-face. Isn't it wonderful to know that God is looking forward to that day as eagerly as any expectant mother?

THOUGHT TO PONDER

❀ Does knowing that God the Son is eagerly anticipating His second coming make it harder or easier to live a full life on this earth?

"The first thing which I can record concerning myself is, that I was born. These are wonderful words. This life, to which neither time nor eternity can bring diminution—this everlasting living soul, began. My mind loses itself in these depths."
—Margaret Oliphant, British writer, 1828-1897

A CHILD'S GARDEN

Children love gardens! They love just about everything about gardens: the shiny tools, the pretty packets of seeds, digging in the dirt, playing in the water, and catching worms. Most of all, they enjoy spending time with Mom or Dad, doing something important. Setting aside a small spot for a child's garden is one of the most rewarding projects parents can engage in with their children. Here are some ideas to make your garden project a successful one:

❀ **Seeds.** Planting a garden from seeds is especially rewarding. Large seeds, such as sunflowers, peas, or nasturtiums, are easiest for little hands to handle. It's tempting to buy a wide variety, but starting with one or two will be more manageable in the long run as regular watering and weeding become necessary.

❀ **Seedlings.** If it's a little late for starting seeds, buying seedlings from a local nursery can be a lot of fun too. Again, keep it simple—just a few plants—so the children will not become overwhelmed caring for them. Let them pick a favorite vegetable or flower. Remember, this is their project. They will develop a lot of pride as they take ownership.

❀ **Garden Beds.** Either a small plot or a large container will work, but you need to make sure that the soil is adequately fertilized, drains well, and gets five to six hours of sunlight a day.

Are We Having Fun Yet?

Finding out you are expecting is one thing. Experiencing the glorious pageant of pregnancy symptoms is another thing altogether! Morning sickness (and there's a misnomer if there ever was one!), cravings, fatigue, back pain, insomnia, decreased bladder capacity, and crying jags—and that's just if we're having a healthy pregnancy. Migraines, high blood pressure, water retention, pregnancy-onset diabetes, anemia, leg cramps, and muscle spasms are fairly common health problems that can be associated with pregnancy. And then there is the emotional anxiety. Will my baby be OK? How will I cope with labor and delivery? Will I be a good mother? Can I really do this? Great expectations and overwhelming anxiety are the stuff all pregnancies are made of. It helps if we have an understanding partner. But most men, even really good and loving men, have some difficulty appreciating the enormous physical, hormonal, and emotional changes that sweep through our bodies. Pregnancy can feel very isolating. But we are not alone. Our Creator God knows and understands every subtle change in body and mood that we are experiencing. He is watching carefully over us. No mater what happens, He is there with us. There are no guarantees of perfection in a sinful world, but He gives us the ultimate guarantee: "I will allow nothing to happen to you that you would not chose if you could see the end from the beginning the way I do. Trust in Me. I can be trusted. I will give you strength and grace for whatever lies ahead. I love you and I love your baby. I would empty heaven to bring you both safely into eternity. I would sacrifice My own child for the eternal redemption of yours."

THOUGHTS TO PONDER

❀ Can I trust God with all areas of my life, including the health and welfare of my children?

❀ Are there some areas of my life that I desire to withhold from God's will?

"Pains of love be sweeter far / Than all the other pleasures are."
—John Dryden, British poet, 1631-1700

AN EXERCISE IN TRUST

We are all familiar with the popular group-therapy exercise of falling backward into the arms of strangers. Supposedly real breakthroughs result with this exercise of trust in a safe, well-controlled environment. Are you prepared to fall backward into the arms of God? Are you ready to let go of all your expectations and say, "Thy will be done"? How tempting to say, "I trust You, God. Now this is what I expect from You."

Dr. Jan Paulsen, president of the Seventh-day Adventist world church, recalls his response when his adult son fell some twenty feet in a construction accident. As his son lay in a coma for two and a half weeks, a grief-stricken father confronted God. "I am carrying on Your work all over the world, Lord. The least I expected was for You to look after my children. I don't think You have done Your job very well!" Dr. Paulsen points out that in all of our lives, there are times we find it very difficult to trust God. We want to tell God what we expect from Him. We want to cut deals. But when we allow ourselves to fall into the arms of grace, we find that He is able to turn our darkest moments into victories.

If you are very brave, list on a sheet of paper the things that you are most reluctant to relinquish entirely to God's will. Is it your children, your marriage, your career, your future? Whatever it is, it will stand between you and God until you accept that God can be trusted with even your most precious and intimate hopes and dreams and relationships. Present your list prayerfully to God. Fall completely into the arms of grace and allow God to work His miracles in your life.

Elephantine

I'm always amazed at stories of young women giving birth in secret, with friends and family never realizing they were pregnant. That certainly wasn't my experience. By the time the eighth month rolls around, most of us have lost visual contact with our feet. It's a mystery why a six-pound infant comes packaged in thirty pounds of excess maternal body weight. By the time Baby is ready to come, we feel as frustrated and helpless as a beetle flipped on its back. It feels uncomfortable to sit, stand, or lie down. Easy chores, such as pulling on socks, require the dexterity of a gymnast. Other young mothers can't resist smiling at our discomfort and advising us to enjoy the peace and quiet because once the baby is born, it's going to get much, much harder. Yes, we know—but wouldn't it be nice to put Baby down for five minutes while we vacuumed under the table!

Have you ever wondered about biblical mothers during their pregnancies? How in the world did ninety-nine-year-old Sarah or post-menopausal Elizabeth manage those last few months? God must have graced them with a youthfulness that transcended their chronological ages. Or what about the teenage Mary astride a donkey for several days' journey at the end of her term? I can't even imagine. Long car trips made me unbearably cranky when I was "great with child." Even God understands the great burden pregnant women carry. In His sermon about the end of the age, Jesus noted, "How dreadful it will be in those days for pregnant women and nursing mothers!" (Matthew 24:19). Our friends and family may grow tired of hearing us complain about our discomfort, but our heavenly Father never dismisses our discomfort. We are privileged for a few short months to share in the creative process with the Creator as life spins and expands within our fertile bodies. He understands better than anyone else what that means.

THOUGHT TO PONDER

❀ New mothers often receive a lot of help and attention. Have I considered what I might do to assist and encourage a mother-to-be?

"Of all the needs (there are none imaginary) a lonely child has, the one that must be satisfied, if there is going to be hope and a hope of wholeness, is the unshaken need for an unshakable God."—Maya Angelou, poet

BEARING ONE ANOTHER'S BURDENS

Each year thousands of unwanted pregnancies end in sadness and tragedy. You don't have to go far to hear stories of abortions, abandoned infants, and abused babies. What can we do about such an enormous and complex problem? Quite a lot, as it turns out. Consider some of the ways you can help. Together we can certainly make a difference! We must.

1. **Legitimacy.** In God's eyes, all children are legitimate. All children deserve to be welcomed, loved, and nurtured. Your attitude makes a difference.
2. **Judgment.** We are nobody's judge. Lectures on the benefits of abstinence, birth control, and sexual morality have a place. They are of no benefit, however, to a pregnant woman. All pregnant women need our full moral support and assistance.
3. **Assistance.** There are many programs, ranging from childcare training to vocational counseling, designed to assist young mothers in the care of their babies. What can you do to help?
4. **Adoption.** Sometimes circumstances preclude a birth mother from rearing her baby. Has God impressed you to consider adoption or foster parenting?
5. **Inclusion.** As members of the body of Christ, all children in the church are our responsibility. What can you do to encourage, nurture, and affirm the children in your church?

Nesting

At some point in most pregnancies, an almost overwhelming urge to "nest" kicks in. Even women who rarely concern themselves with décor are surprised to find that they are suddenly developing a keen interest in coordinating baby-crib linens and in stenciling techniques. Those of us who love decorating are plunged into a near frenzy of decorating mania. Whether you found yourself painting everything that wasn't moving or survived the nesting instinct by applying an adhesive wall border, you know what I'm talking about. The baby is coming, and a certain urgency asserts itself. Little jammies fill the drawers. Stacks of impossibly tiny diapers and baby powder sit on the changer. Soft cuddly animals are propped about the room. All wait expectantly for the arrival of the little prince or princess. Somewhere in heaven I think God is looking down upon us and smiling. He has prepared a place for us, and He is waiting for our arrival. Someday soon He, too, will bring us home.

"In my Father's house are many rooms; if it were not so, I would have told you. I am going there to prepare a place for you. And if I go and prepare a place for you, I will come back and take you to be with me that you also may be where I am" (John 14:2, 3).

THOUGHTS TO PONDER

❀ Do we get so wrapped up on this earth that we sometimes forget that heaven waits for us?

❀ Does God anticipate our homecoming as keenly as we anticipate the homecoming of our children?

"You can dream, create, design and build the most wonderful place in the world, but it requires people to make the dream a reality."—Walt Disney

HEIRLOOMS

The next time you are searching for a gift for a special baby, consider passing on a special heirloom. Following are some items that may be languishing in your attic or basement that could become a treasured heirloom to be passed on again.

❀ **Vintage Hanky Bonnets.** Pretty handkerchiefs used to be *de rigueur* for all properly dressed ladies. Now out of style, they are easily fashioned into lovely infant bonnets.

❀ **Old Doll Clothes.** Either handmade or vintage, old doll clothes make beautiful gifts to hang on the wall or to dress little teddy bears with.

❀ **Children's Books.** Do you have some beloved children's books that were read over and over again? Tie up a small pile of them with a pretty ribbon, and new memories will begin again.

❀ **Embroidered Pillowcases.** Years ago, embroidering was a very popular craft. The pillowcases make charming nursery decorations.

❀ **Hand-me-down Toys.** Although very old toys are often not safe to play with anymore, they make delightful nursery decorations and often encourage family stories about the original owners.

❀ **Vintage Children's Furniture.** Any wooden children's furniture that predates pressboard and laminate makes a treasured heirloom. Little chairs, tables, and high chairs are particularly charming. PLEASE make sure that all items meet current safety standards. If in doubt, check with consumer safety guidelines such as <www.safetyalerts.com>.

The Agony and the Ecstasy

Finally it happens! The pain is more than a stitch in the side. The contractions are leaving no doubts about being the real thing! In fact, you no longer care whether it's the real thing or not; you just want it to stop. That's the real thing. It's time to go to the hospital. If someone can get your focal point and your lollypops in the car, wonderful, but for heaven's sake, step on it! The birthing classes made this agony sound so bearable—as if it could be controlled with good thoughts and deep breathing. It can't. Whatever made you think that six weeks of classes could turn you into a Zen master, capable of walking across hot coals in your bare feet and leaping tall buildings in a single bound? This hurts like hell. What the nurse is referring to blithely as "discomfort" makes you wish she was "uncomfortable" too. At some point, the whole process resolves itself, and you find yourself holding a tiny red-and-pink creature. As the little lips nuzzle instinctively against you for nourishment and the small fingers wrap tightly around your own, you realize with a shock that you'd do it all over again. Who knew it would be like this? The agony and the ecstasy, the great creative process!

THOUGHTS TO PONDER
- Is it possible to consider that the pain of this life will be resolved someday?
- How do I trust in God's goodness when I am experiencing great pain?

"A woman giving birth to a child has pain because her time has come; but when her baby is born she forgets the anguish because of her joy. . . . So with you: Now is your time of grief, but I will see you again and you will rejoice, and no one will take away your joy."
—Jesus Christ

THE CREATIVE PROCESS

In the famous movie *The Agony and the Ecstasy*, the master artist Michelangelo struggles to complete his great masterpiece on the Sistine Chapel ceiling. All creative projects, even if they are not as grand as the Sistine Chapel ceiling, have their moments of intense agony. If you're in the midst of a creative process, whether it's completing a degree, writing a book, composing music, or reorganizing a Sabbath School program, consider the following:

1. In the process of every creative project, you will lose confidence in it. In fact, you may decide that you absolutely loathe the entire idea. As I tell my art students, this is perfectly normal and to be expected. Just keep moving.
2. At some point, you are going to experience a serious creative block. You will feel stupid, incompetent, untalented, and completely unable to resolve the project. This is also normal. You are not stupid, incompetent, or lacking in talent. You are experiencing creative labor pains. Just keep moving.
3. Before the process is complete, you will be tempted to abandon it. The initial flush of creative energy has evaporated. You are left with a ton of work to plough through. Have faith that you can make it happen. Just keep moving.
4. Finish the details. As you get nearer to completion, it is tempting to start cutting corners. Take a deep breath and bear down. This is the final stretch. Stay focused and just keep moving.
5. At some point in every creative project, it is finished. It is time to step back, pat yourself on the back, and enjoy the fruits of your labor. You may feel reluctant to let go and want to go back and keep editing, adding, and refining. This is also perfectly normal. But now is the time to move on. Congratulations!

Here's Looking at You Kid

My first child was born back in the "dark ages" when babies were whisked away the moment they were born, and efficient nurses would bring them to the mother's bed every four hours for a "visit." I recall the first moments alone with my new daughter. She was in a receiving blanket, wrapped tighter than a Vienna sausage. Her little head was covered in a cap. I could see nothing except her tiny puckered face. The nurse laid her on my lap with a brisk, "I'll leave you to it." It . . . ? I really had no clue what to do with "it." We were alone for the very first time. I gazed at the baby lying on my lap for several minutes, wondering what was expected of me. I'd barely gotten a glimpse of her in the delivery room. For nine months I had been wondering what she would look like, and now, here she was. Almost hesitantly, I began to carefully unwrap the layers of blankets and clothing. She seemed so delicate and breakable. I marveled at her tiny, tiny fingers and toes and almost transparent fingernails. I slipped off her cap, and I could see the small blue veins pulsating beneath her soft dark hair. I carefully examined her navel clip, so bloody and blue, already turning black—the place we had been connected just hours before.

Suddenly her little face began to pucker, and she pulled her soft dimpled knees up to her stomach and began to cry. I lifted her awkwardly to my chest, and within moments we'd taught each other what we needed to know about nursing. As babies and mothers have taught each other from the dawn of time. "Here's looking at you kid," I said out loud. "I think this could be the beginning of a beautiful friendship."

THOUGHT TO PONDER

❀ Is it just me, or is the Creator never more fully revealed than in the marvelous intricacy of a newborn infant?

"I praise you because I am fearfully and wonderfully made; your works are wonderful, I know that full well" (Psalm 139:14).

GARDEN SPINACH LASAGNA
FRESH PRODUCE

This recipe calls for garden-fresh spinach. If you're not growing it, pick some up at the produce market. Preparation time: approximately 30 minutes. Baking time: 30-40 minutes. Serves 12.

Pantry Items
Egg noodles (1 16-oz. package)
Olive oil (2 Tbsp.)
Oregano (1/2 tsp.)
Nutmeg (1/2 tsp.)
Dill (1/2 tsp.)
Chicken-style seasoning (2 Tbsp.)

Fresh Items
Fresh spinach
   (4 cups, packed)
Onion (1)
Garlic (3 cloves)
Eggs (4)
Sour cream (1/2 cup)
Ricotta cheese (1 1/2 cups)
Fresh grated Parmesan cheese (3/4 cup)

DIRECTIONS
Cook egg noodles according to package directions, rinse, and drain. Meanwhile, carefully wash and drain spinach and lay on paper towels to dry. Dice onion and mince garlic; sauté in olive oil over medium-low heat until onion is softened. Add spinach and toss gently until spinach is just wilted; remove from heat. In a large mixing bowl, combine eggs, ricotta cheese, sour cream, oregano, nutmeg, dill, and chicken-style seasoning. Fold in egg noodles and sautéed spinach mixture. Pour into 4-quart casserole dish. Top with Parmesan cheese. May cover and refrigerate overnight. Before baking, bring to room temperature. Bake 30 to 40 minutes at 350° F.

Love Poured Out in a Child

When we hold our babies in our arms, our bodies surge with powerful maternal instincts. Woe to the man, woman, or beast that would attempt to harm our beloved child. Is there anything we wouldn't do to protect our little ones from danger? Of course not! These children entrusted to our care are woven into our very hearts. They are the expression of our best intentions, our deepest hopes, and our purest dreams. The essence of love is poured out in a child. As we hold our children, we are reminded that it was through divine love poured out in the Christ Child that humankind was redeemed. What must it have been like to be chosen, as Mary was, to be the mother of the Baby Jesus? As I've hoped and dreamed for my children, I have considered how unfair it must have been to be selected to give birth to a child whose destiny it was to become the Messiah, the Lamb of God, the divine Sacrifice. It wasn't a job Mary signed up for. I'm sure it wasn't a job Mary wanted. And how she endured that agonizing task I have no idea, but I am so grateful and thankful that she not only endured it but also embraced that terrible responsibility with all her heart. By becoming a willing instrument of God's will, she became a part of the plan of salvation. In a small way, every mother is given the same mission. By becoming willing instruments of God's will, we surrender our children to God's plans, not our own. Only through letting go of our own wants, desires, and dreams for our children can we become the instruments of their of salvation. We have an awesome task ahead of us. By the grace of God we can see it through.

THOUGHTS TO PONDER

❀ Can I grasp the fact that God's plans for my children greatly transcend my highest human dreams?

❀ Am I willing to completely support my children as God leads in their lives?

"Man's ultimate destiny is to become one with the Divine Power which governs and sustains the creation and its creatures."—Alfred A. Montapert

PAMPER BASKET
INSIDE ACTIVITY

Ages: 5 and up
Materials Needed:
  Dollar-store baskets
  Tissue paper
  Ribbon
  Assorted personal-care travel-size items

This very simple project yields very impressive results for little hands, but it does require some advance planning on your part. You will need to visit a drug store or dollar store to purchase a handful of personal-care items such as soap, shampoo, perfume, body sponges, bath beads, etc. Help your children line the basket with one or two sheets of tissue paper. Arrange the items in the basket and tie with a big bow. If you want to make it extra fancy, place each item in the middle of a square of tissue paper and pull up the edges and tie with a ribbon, bon-bon style. It makes for a very festive-looking basket. These pamper baskets, along with a handmade note, make wonderful gifts for moms, grandmas, babysitters, convalescents, and neighbors.

Sleeping Like a Baby

During the first week home with a new baby, you have to wonder where the term "sleeping like a baby" came from. A birth mother certainly didn't coin it. If she had, it would mean something entirely different from the way the phrase is commonly used. A new baby usually means that nobody in the house is getting very much sleep. You would throw yourself in front of a grizzly bear for your new bundle of joy, but you just don't know whether you can manage one more 3:00 A.M. feeding and still hang on to that last scrap of sanity. Nights blur into days. Sleep deprivation does funny things to your sense of time. You ask yourself silly questions such as, "Is the sun setting or rising?" And if there are toddlers in the house to care for as well, a new mother performs under conditions that make Special Forces training look like child's play. It feels like a marathon in endurance—it pretty much is. Until finally, miracle of miracles, your baby sleeps through the night! As dawn breaks, you rush into the baby's room to make sure all is well. It is. The child is sleeping quietly, all snuggled up in the crib, her little chest raising and falling rhythmically. The baby looks like an angel. Birds are singing. Flowers are blooming. Somewhere a baby is crying, but it's not yours. Yours is sleeping like a baby. Life is good!

THOUGHTS TO PONDER

❀ Life is full of everyday blessings. Do I ever take a moment to cherish them?

❀ Children come and go in our lives so quickly. Am I making a point to enjoy them while I can?

"There never was a child so lovely, but his mother was glad to get him asleep."
—*Ralph Waldo Emerson*

EDIBLE FLOWER GARDEN

Flowers are beautiful to look at. But did you know that many of them are delicious and nutritious as well? Edible flowers are a gourmet's delight. They add a delightful touch to otherwise ordinary recipes and make special dishes extraordinary. It is much safer to grow your own edible flowers than to use flowers grown in a commercial nursery because of the chemicals and pesticides used. It is also important to treat edible flowers as you would any produce from your garden and to rinse them well before using. If you are thinking about growing your own edible flower garden, following are a few suggestions:

- ❀ **Roses.** Roses have long been used in teas and infusions. Rose petals can also be used to add delicate ornamentation to cakes and desserts. Gently remove the rose petals and rinse them in a bath of cold water. Lay the petals on paper towels to dry. To enhance their appearance, spray them with vegetable oil cooking spray and/or sprinkle them with fine granular sugar.
- ❀ **Pansies.** Pansies can be treated much as you would roses except that the petals can be left intact. They do not have to be removed if you rinse the flowers well.
- ❀ **Dandelions.** Young dandelion greens make a wonderful early spring salad. Flowers need to be rinsed especially well to remove soil and insects before adding to salad.
- ❀ **Nasturtiums.** These bright flowers and their leaves have a sharp peppery taste that goes especially well with salads and in sandwiches. Use nasturtiums to decorate potatoes, pasta, and garden salads. They will also add a wonderful finishing touch to open-face sandwiches.
- ❀ **Marigolds.** These flowers are sometimes called the "poor man's saffron." A handful of the center petals from bright gold and orange marigolds can be minced and added to cooking rice to produce a beautiful saffronlike yellow.

Lead Me Beside Still Waters

Psalm 23 was probably the first Bible passage you memorized. With its soft, pastoral images, Psalm 23 is very comforting. That's how we like to encourage children to picture Jesus, as the gentle Good Shepherd, cradling the little lambs in His strong arms. But we're big girls now, aren't we?

When was the last time we allowed the Good Shepherd to lead us anywhere? Life is lived at such a fast pace. Each day is a marathon of responsibilities and duties. When our head finally hits the pillow at night, there is little energy left to linger by still waters and cool pools, no matter how inviting. We're just happy if we can make it through the night without waking up to a nagging list of worries at 2:00 A.M. But wouldn't it be nice if there were a quiet oasis, a place to restore our soul, to soothe our troubled hearts, a place where big girls could go to feel safe and warm and refreshed? O dear Father, heal us of our addictions. Rescue us from the rapids we live in. Set us beside the still waters.

He leads me beside quiet waters, he restores my soul (Psalm 23:2, 3).

THOUGHTS TO PONDER
❀ David wrote Psalm 23 while fleeing from Saul. Is my life really more hectic than his?
❀ How can I claim Psalm 23 for me, today, in my busy life?

"The one important thing I have learned over the years is the difference between taking one's work seriously and taking one's self seriously. The first is imperative and the second is disastrous."—Margot Fonteyn

BALANCE AND BOUNDARIES

Is your life out of balance? Do you feel guilty about it? How would you put balance back into your life? Would you have to say No to somebody? Would that make you feel even more guilty? Dr. Susan Irish-Zelener, a clinical psychologist in Loma Linda, California, contends that Adventist women as a group tend to chronically neglect self-care. As a result, many Adventist women suffer from obesity, poor health, depression, and anxiety. Our inability to set healthy boundaries compromises our ability to live well and love well. Believing that we are at the bottom of the totem pole, that we are the last ones to have our needs met, is not biblical. If we do not love and nurture ourselves, we cannot effectively nurture others. We cannot draw from an empty well. I have known busy women who take care of themselves. It is not a contradiction in terms. It is not an impossible task. In fact, it is a life-critical task. How would you respond to the following questions? (I bet you already know the right answers.)

Do I take time for self-care activities every day?
   A. What exactly would a self-care activity look like?
   B. Every once in a while I make an effort at prayer journaling or exercise.
   C. Taking care of myself helps me be a better wife, mother, and businesswoman.

Do I spend at least an hour a week exploring my own interests?
   A. Yes, if that includes grocery shopping.
   B. I used to have outside interests, but now I wait for vacations to enjoy them.
   C. I don't consider it selfish to reserve at least an hour a week to pursue personal interests.

Where Have All the Cowboys Gone?

You've heard the song "Where Have All the Cowboys Gone?" We live in such a graceless age. The gas-station attendant doesn't pump your gas anymore. You're not even sure you can trust him to check your oil and give you a level answer. Where's John Wayne when you need him?

I met a cowboy once. We were on a camping trip in the middle of Montana, and our VW bus broke down. Luckily, we were able to coast down to a small town. It was late on a Friday afternoon. The only garage in town was closed. At the café next door we were told that the mechanic would be back in the morning. An old cowboy offered to take us up to his place for the evening. Of course we declined, but he was persistent. He said his wife kept a "travelers' room" for unexpected guests. We were hot and tired, and it sounded too good to be true. The cowboy drove us several miles to a cottage nestled against the side of the mountain. His wife seemed happy to see us even though it was late. True to his word, the "travelers' room" was waiting with fresh linens and towels. The next morning, after a huge breakfast, we toured the cowboy's "ranch." It wasn't big. He told us he worked as a cowhand in a big outfit in the valley. It was his dream to build up a small herd of his own. He had about a dozen head so far. As we were admiring them, a large pickup hauling a huge vat pulled into the yard. Several men jumped out and headed for the barn. The old cowboy looked confused. We were even more so. Amid all the hub-bub, we finally learned that the rancher in the valley had sent his son and several ranch hands up with a dipping bath to dip the fledgling herd so any parasites on his animals would be destroyed. The old man's face was wet with tears, and he had a huge grin.

That's been my only experience with cowboys, and I'd sure like to know, where have all the cowboys gone?

THOUGHTS TO PONDER

❀ In these times is it still possible to bestow acts of kindness upon strangers?

❀ Is the art of hospitality a dying art?

"I was hungry and you gave me something to eat . . . I was a stranger and you invited me in."
—*Jesus Christ*

MY COWBOY

Is there a special man in your life who's been there for you during tough times? Someone who seems to know without asking what you need? Someone who goes out on a limb for you and always supports you? If you're lucky, you know someone like that— your father, an uncle, a brother, your husband. Cowboys aren't always expressive. They let their actions do the talking, but if you think they're not suckers for a romantic gesture, you'd be mistaken. Do something extravagantly romantic for your cowboy this week. After all, cowboys are hard to find—and they're worth it!

❀ A rose with a note will make a cowboy weak in the knees.
❀ A mushy card from you will probably be saved forever.
❀ A small gift, wrapped and left on his desk or workbench, will leave him misty-eyed.

Give Me Peace and Prosperity

Francis Schaeffer, the famous Christian apologist, observed that as Christian-dominated values have waned in Western culture, they have been replaced with the universal ideals of personal peace and affluence. Schaeffer defines the philosophy of personal peace as "wanting to have my personal life pattern undisturbed in my lifetime," a desire not to be troubled by the troubles of other people or other generations. "Affluence means an overwhelming and ever-increasing prosperity—a life made up of things, things, and more things."

Peace and prosperity, what could be wrong with that? Isn't that the great American dream? Isn't that why thousands of immigrants have thronged our shores? Isn't that the promise we hold out to a world wracked with want and war? Perhaps there's nothing wrong with peace and prosperity if I'm willing to fight for it for my neighbor. Perhaps Schaeffer is saying there's a lot wrong if the focus of my life is an insurance of peace and prosperity for me and my family. Such subtle shifts in view. How easily we can be seduced by the desire for peace and prosperity.

THOUGHTS TO PONDER

❀ How can I help alleviate want and violence in my own community?
❀ Have I considered what my responsibilities might be as a citizen of the world?

"If ye love wealth greater than liberty, the tranquility of servitude greater than the animating contest for freedom, go home from us in peace. We seek not your counsel, nor your arms. Crouch down and lick the hand that feeds you. May your chains set lightly upon you, and may posterity forget that ye were our countrymen."—Samuel Adams

CHRISTIAN CHARITY

As blessed as we are in a country where even our poorest citizens are offered food and shelter, it is easy to forget that thousands of families around the world are languishing in extreme poverty and want. Seventh-day Adventists have a long history of outreach to underprivileged people around our globe. Have you every considered a missionary trip in place of a family vacation? Would it be possible for your family to participate in one of the following outreach programs?

❈ Adventist Development and Relief Agency International—<www.adra.org>.
❈ Adventist Volunteer Service—<http://volunteers.gc.adventist.org>.
❈ Be a Missionary—<www.adventist.org/beamissionary>.
❈ Total Employment—<www.totalemployment.org>.
❈ The Center for Youth Evangelism—<www.andrews.edu/CFYE>.
❈ Doctors Without Borders—<www.doctorswithoutborders.org>.

Give Me Your Tired, Your Poor—NOT!

Pastor Maggie Wise recently delivered a sermon to the Judson Memorial Church in New York City with the above title. Studying for her master of divinity degree at the New York Theological Seminary, Pastor Wise had just completed a group research project on the detention of immigrants. Working in view of the Statue of Liberty on which Emma Lazarus's famous poem is inscribed, Pastor Wise's research shocked her so deeply that, in her words, "my religion was shaken to its roots."

To get them started, The NYTS group was provided with the case study of a Sri Lanka family requesting asylum. Pastor Wise assumed that the circumstances endured by the Sri Lanka family were grossly exaggerated for the

purposes of the study. A tour of a nearby detention center changed her mind. The detention center, run by a for-profit corporation, housed immigrants seeking asylum in large warehouses with forty individuals to a room, open toilets, and small exercise areas roofed in wire mesh. Treated like criminals with few of the legal rights of criminals, families fleeing from almost certain death are locked up sometimes for four years in these harsh conditions before their requests for asylum are even heard. I can't imagine what it would be like to be so afraid for my family's safety that I would willingly subject them to such treatment on just a hope—because hope was all I had left to offer them.

THOUGHTS TO PONDER
- Our country has a strong, proud history of providing asylum to oppressed people. What has caused the shift in our nation's focus?
- What responsibility do I have to protect those who cannot protect themselves?

"I was a stranger and you did not invite me in. . . . Whatever you did not do for one of the least of these, you did not do for me."—Jesus Christ

PREJUDICE

In Christ there is neither Jew nor Greek, slave nor free, male nor female. Still, living in a sinful world, I've heard devout Christians utter the most despicable racial slurs without so much as a blush. I've listened to the ugly sound track in my own mind, reacting in fear or ignorance or anger to the actions of someone who does not look like me. The seeds of prejudice are virulent, sending roots to the very core of who we are, choking out the possibility for real fellowship with our brothers and sisters in Christ. Can we fight such an overwhelming force as prejudice in our work, our families, our church? Can we ask ourselves the tough questions?

- ❀ Is my worst personal prejudice racial, economic, cultural, or intellectual?
- ❀ Do I make an effort to appreciate the cultural differences expressed in worship in my church?
- ❀ Does our family socialize with families of various ethnic backgrounds?
- ❀ When I see prejudice at work, at church, or at home, how do I respond?
- ❀ What do my words, actions, and expressions tell my children about how I really feel?

Where the Buffalo Roam

Oh, give me a home, where the buffalo roam,
Where the deer and the antelope play. . . .

Weaving in and out of rush-hour traffic on any given workday, one hand on the wheel, the other balancing the travel mug, autodialing the office from the headset, successfully cutting off the sod buster in the pickup trying to change lanes! This is not multitasking for amateurs; this is the stuff true road warriors are made of, with places to be and people to see. Addicted to our own adrenalin rush. Addicted? You bet!

What would we do with a home where the deer and the antelope play, where seldom is heard a discouraging word, and the skies are not cloudy all day? Wouldn't that be great? No meetings, no deadlines, no appointments. No secretaries, no clients, no staff. Sounds like heaven, doesn't it? Perhaps it is, but how many of us are ready to give up our clout, affluence, and just plain old importance for heaven? The rush might be more addictive than we think.

THOUGHTS TO PONDER

❀ Do I sometimes get restless on the weekends, eager for Monday to roll back around?
❀ When was the last time I sat quietly with God, listening to the still, small voice?

"He that can take rest is greater than he that can take cities."—Benjamin Franklin

OATMEAL-NUT PATTIES
VEGETARIAN ALTERNATIVE

These easy vegetarian burgers are a delicious and healthful substitute for the real thing. Makes 4 generous burger-size patties. Doubles easily for a group. Preparation time: 10 minutes. Baking time: 20 minutes.

Pantry Items
Oatmeal (2 cups)
Bisquick baking mix (1/2 cup)
Onion soup mix (1 packet)
Ketchup (1 Tbsp.)
Walnuts (1/2 cup, chopped)

Fresh Items
Eggs (2)
Cottage cheese (1 cup)
Fresh mushrooms (1 cup, coarsely chopped)
Fresh garlic (2 cloves)
Fresh rosemary (1 tsp., chopped)

DIRECTIONS
Preheat oven to 400° F. Chop nuts, mushrooms, rosemary, and garlic. In a large bowl, mix all ingredients. Form mixture into 3-inch patties. Place patties on a lightly greased cookie sheet and bake in the oven for 20 minutes. When done, the center of the patty will spring back when lightly depressed with the back of a fork. Serve on buns accompanied by relish tray of sprouts, lettuce, tomatoes, onions, and condiments.

ALTERNATIVES
You may substitute 1 cup of firm tofu for the cottage cheese. If your family enjoys vegetables, experiment by chopping and adding one of the following to the burger mixture: black olives, zucchini, or dried tomatoes.

Purple Mountains Majesty

Before the mountains were settled in place, before the hills, I was given birth (Proverbs 8:25.)

If you've ever stood in the midst of the Rocky Mountains, you know what it is to understand your own insignificance. The sheer impact of those towering peaks, one next to the other as far as the eye can see, is magnificent and humbling at the same moment. I have an agnostic friend who likes to debate the existence of God. One day we were comparing unforgettable moments. My friend chose a moment he experienced on a business trip, sitting in a restaurant patio overlooking the Rocky Mountains. "I don't know how to explain it," he confided, "but as I looked out over those mountains, I felt like we were not alone. Like I was not alone. I almost believed in God. I sat there for a very long time." My friend, whoever does not believe in God, has heard Him speak. The Creator God speaks to us through the terrible majesty of His creation. One must vigilantly maintain a constant hum of activity to drown out the sound of His voice.

THOUGHTS TO PONDER
- Have I experienced the "Sabbath Rest" God desires to give me?
- How can I share the magnificence of God's creation with my children?

"Faith is to believe what we do not see, and the reward of this faith is to see what we believe."—St. Augustine

VISIT TO THE ZOO
SUNNY DAY ACTIVITY

Ages: 2 to Adult
Materials Needed:
- Sun hat
- Water bottles
- Sunscreen
- Camera
- Wet wipes
- Snacks (for the kids, not the animals)

Kids of all ages enjoy a trip to the zoo! Sabbath is a perfect day to explore the wonders of creation. Face to face with the marvelous diversity of animal life, it is difficult to ignore the awesome imagination of the Creator! A few **"ZOO Tips"** to make the day an enjoyable one for the entire family:

- ❀ **Zoos Can Get Hot.** Don't forget water and sun protection!
- ❀ **Map Out Your Safari.** Zoos can be overwhelming. Don't try to see the whole zoo in one day.
- ❀ **Buy a Seasonal Zoo Pass.** Most zoos offer seasonal passes you can purchase ahead of time, allowing you unlimited access to the zoo, even to other nature attractions such as aquariums and planetariums.
- ❀ **Check Out the Picnic Areas.** Some zoos have beautiful picnic areas, great for a picnic lunch or snack to break up the afternoon.

Amber Fields of Grain

"A farmer went out to sow his seed . . ." begins Christ's parable of a farmer scattering grain across his freshly plowed fields, anticipating a rich harvest. Amber fields of ripening grain swaying in the sun. As one of the world's foremost wheat-producing nations, we have sometimes been called the "bread basket of the world." What wonderful imagery of golden fields and fresh-baked bread. Like goodness itself, warm and nurturing. That's the way we like to think of ourselves when we sing "America the Beautiful" in those moments of patriotic pride and remembrance—wholesome, generous, abundant. And if any nation has to pick an image to live up to, what could be better than that? For all our faults, our failures, our shortcomings, and our excesses, we are still one of the most generous nations on earth. We truly want to help. We line up to give our blood, our time, our talent, our money. If our efforts are clumsy or heavy handed or inadequate at times, it is not because our hearts are not in the right place. Like the farmer in Christ's parable, some of the seeds fall by the wayside and some on stony ground and hearts. Then we reap an unexpected harvest of hatred, resentment, and suspicion that sends us reeling. Is that reason enough to withold our generosity? I don't think so. So far America hasn't thought so either. "America! America! / God shed his grace on thee; / And crown thy good with brotherhood / From sea to shining sea."

THOUGHTS TO PONDER

❀ Do I sometimes refrain from helping because I fear being misunderstood?

❀ Do I sometimes refrain from giving because I fear my money will be misused?

"America is a willingness of the heart."—*F. Scott Fitzgerald*

INVESTMENT PROJECTS

Do you remember Sabbath School Investment projects? Those quarterly Sabbath School projects to raise money for missions? Maybe you saved pennies and spare change. Maybe you raked yards for a quarter. Perhaps your dad helped you plant vegetables on a small patch in the family garden, to grow and sell for your investment project.

Have you heard about Amazing Maisie? Maisie DeVore gets the "Mother of all Investment Projects Award." In 1971, Maisie DeVore set about raising money for a community pool for the children in her small Kansas town. She started by collecting aluminum cans. For years she combed dumpsters and roadsides for cans. When it was too cold to hunt cans, Maisie knitted afghans to sell at flea markets. As she grew older, her children became concerned about her obsession with the community swimming pool and tried to get her to donate the money she'd already collected to another cause and cease her endless trekking for cans. Maisie refused to be deterred. By the turn of the century, to everyone's surprise, eighty-one-year-old Maisie had collected $100,000 toward her project! The state of Kansas added $73,000, and on July 14, 2001—thirty years after Maisie began her little investment project—the Eskridge, Kansas, Community Swimming Pool officially opened.

There's something very gratifying and character building about working hard to benefit someone else. There is a lot of talk these days about instilling self-esteem in our children. I'm not sure it is possible to instill self-esteem in children, but I do believe you can encourage them to develop it for themselves. Is there an investment project your family could get behind?

WEEK 9 — MONDAY

A Promised Land

The Israelites knew they had finally escaped the bondage of Egypt when they watched the mighty Egyptian chariots being swept into the Red Sea. Miriam broke out the tambourines and led the Israelites in a rousing song and dance. They were finally on their way! Oh how good it felt to be traveling toward the Promised Land, the land flowing with milk and honey. Of course, journeys are often unpredictable—and the Exodus certainly was. After wandering in circles in the desert for what must have seemed an interminably long time, the children of Israel finally made it to the border. Now what? The produce was certainly lovely if you could overlook the troublesome giants. A lot of grumbling ensued, and almost everybody wished they were back in the "old country." Apparently the hot sun had addled their memory of whips and chains.

The journey to the Promised Land is one of the great archetypical stories in literature, the search for a better place, a better future. The story is retold in a hundred variations. It always ends the same, however. The Promised Land never lives up to expectations. It seems that, as humans, we have unlimited capacity for high expectations. Anything less than perfect is a big disappointment. The new church is barely finished and consecrated before the grumbling begins. Construction on the school is hardly begun before the multitude identifies the inherent flaws. Dissatisfaction is always fully matured before the paint is dry. It doesn't matter how awful the old place was because the new place is never perfect. How does God put up with us? Somehow, He marches us along, and in spite of ourselves, after untold miracles, we find ourselves living in the Promised Land. That's the really big miracle!

THOUGHTS TO PONDER

❀ Does my marriage, my kid's school, my job really have to be perfect for me to be happy?

❀ Has my quest for perfection ever cheated me out of a wonderful experience?

"For other nations, utopia is a blessed past never to be recovered; for Americans it is just beyond the horizon."—Henry Kissinger

THE WASTELAND OF PERFECTIONISM

Striving for excellence is dynamic. Perfectionism is crippling. The artist in pursuit of excellence will follow her interests even if it means experimenting with new styles, new techniques, or new subject matter. A perfectionist will become stuck repainting the same pictures over and over and over again. She would call it "perfecting her craft" instead of what it really is, fear of growth. The same could be said for any perfectionist, whether the medium she works with is paint, music, words, or even spirituality. An obsession with perfection is all about self. Prayerfully consider these questions:

- ❀ What in my life needs to be released from the crippling grip of perfectionism?
- ❀ What could I learn if I didn't worry about looking or feeling awkward when I tried?
- ❀ Is my vision of perfection about my work, my home, my family, my friendships, or my spouse hurting relationships I cherish?
- ❀ Can I trust God enough to understand that He has a special work for me to do even though I am not perfect?

Wasteland

The 1922 poem "The Waste Land" is perhaps T. S. Eliot's most famous work. This controversial poem details the journey of modern humanity's search for redemption.

What are the roots that clutch, what branches
     grow
Out of this stony rubbish? Son of man,
You cannot say, or guess, for you know only
A heap of broken images, where the sun beats,
And the dead tree gives no shelter, the cricket
     no relief,
And the dry stone no sound of water. Only
There is shadow under this red rock,
(Come in under the shadow of this red rock),
And I will show you something different from
     either
Your shadow at morning striding behind you
Or your shadow at evening rising to meet you;
I will show you fear in a handful of dust.
—ll 19-30, "The Waste Land"

There are times when we feel broken, barren, and withered. Times when our lives rise before us in "a heap of broken images." Our soul yearns for shelter and relief. According to "The Waste Land," we find instead only "fear in a handful of dust." This world is not our home. Some days that seems perfectly clear.

THOUGHTS TO PONDER
❀ Is God big enough to sustain me through a crisis of faith?
❀ If I doubt God, will He disappear?

"If you're going through hell, keep going."— *Sir Winston Churchill*

WHEN GOD IS NOT THERE

Many Christians believe that depression and discouragement are evidence of a lack of faith. Ashamed and embarrassed, too many Christians suffer silently. But in Scripture we find that faith giants such as Elijah, David, and Moses all experienced serious bouts of discouragement and depression. God is big enough to sustain us even when we doubt. Isn't it time we quit trying to do it all by ourselves? There are places we can go for help:

❀ Local pastors can provide counseling or a referral.
❀ Some organizations provide Christian therapists and counselors. To find a counselor near you, conduct an Internet search using the phrase "Christian Counselor."
❀ Some Christian counselors, such as Barnabus Christian Counseling Network, offer Internet counseling with maximum privacy. Check out <www.barnabus.com>.
❀ Family physicians can offer referrals targeting specific needs.

The Sea Turned to Blood

The second angel sounded his trumpet. . . . A third of the sea turned into blood, a third of the living creatures in the sea died (Revelation 8:8, 9).

As a nation, we produce an enormous volume of garbage. It's quite a dilemma. What do we do with it? "Sylvia Snout, please take the garbage out."—Shel Silverstien. A few years ago, a barge of garbage from New York traveled to six states and three countries in the Caribbean, searching for space in a landfill. It finally returned to New York, where the garbage was incinerated. All sorts of debris have washed up on our beaches, including highly regulated medical waste, plastic infusion bottles, and hypodermic needles. Then there's the small problem of nuclear waste. With a half-life longer than civilization, where do we store it? Can we shoot it into outer space? Suppose it were to fall from the sky?

A few years ago I was interviewing a computer engineer. The nuclear power plant where he worked had closed due to economic infeasibility. He had created a rather ingenious computer model to track the storage of used nuclear canisters resting in a cooling bath. As the engineer proudly unrolled the grid peppered with X's marking the spot, my heart skipped a beat. "How long until these canisters are no longer dangerous?" I asked. "Never, as far as we know," was his casual reply. "What happens if sometime between now and eternity the water in the bath were to warm up a few degrees?" I asked. "Oh, that could never be allowed to happen," was the solemn reply. "But let's say it did," I pressed. "It would probably take out a good part of the state in the explosion. Of course, the entire region would be unlivable for several hundred years. But that would never happen," he assured me again. *Never* seems like a very long time to count on. What human hubris ever persuaded us to create something so catastrophically dangerous that could not be uncreated?

THOUGHTS TO PONDER

❀ Are we compelled to create, simply because we can?

❀ Where do Christians weigh in on the debate between science and ethics?

"For a successful technology, reality must take precedence over public relations, for Nature cannot be fooled."—Richard P. Feynman

RECYCLING

We might not be able to clean up the entire globe, but we can help tidy up a little part of it. Recycling is as good for the soul as for the environment. There is something very satisfying about adding to our resources instead of clogging up our landfills. Chances are your community has a recycling program. If you're not already participating, now is a great time to start.

❀ This is a great site to visit with your kids! Cartoon style, it's fun and informative even for adults. You can get great ideas while playing the clean-up game! Worth the visit! *<http://www.epa.gov/recyclecity>*.

❀ Earth 911. This is an easy-to-navigate, yet comprehensive site of local recycling programs and sites. Just enter your zip code. An excellent community resource! *<http://www.1800cleanup.org>*.

Rivers Ran With Wormwood

The third angel sounded his trumpet, and a great star, blazing like a torch, fell from the sky. . . . The name of the star is Wormwood. A third of the waters turned bitter, and many people died from the waters (Revelation 8:10, 11).

Water is one of our most basic necessities. Science tells us that water is needed to sustain life, any life. Evolutionists regard water as the medium from which all living organisms originated. Recently the discovery of frozen water on Mars has led scientists to speculate that life in some form may have once existed there. Deprived of water, we perish rather quickly.

Water has spiritual significance as well. While He was here on earth, Christ referred to Himself as the Water of Life. In baptism, we are cleansed by the water and the Spirit. Water is universally recognized as a symbol of life and renewal.

Have you ever been revolted by the sight of a polluted stream or river? Perhaps you were hiking in the woods and came across a remote creek clogged with tires, beer cans, and rusting debris. Did you wonder How? Why? Even in the wilderness, our waters are filled with the debris of human waste. Refuse clogs our streams, toxic chemicals bleed into our water supply, hypodermic needles litter our beaches. At the same time, something in the human heart knows that polluting the waters is a sacrilege, an act of evil, a violation of life.

THOUGHTS TO PONDER

❀ Does the company I work for practice responsible ecological procedures?

❀ What steps do I take to preserve the purity of God's creation?

"Nature encourages no looseness, pardons no errors."
—*Ralph Waldo Emerson*

WATER SAFETY

This is the time of year that kids love to swim and play in the water. Whether it's a wading pool, a private pool, community pool, lake, or beach, it's difficult to coax kids out of the water on a warm, sunny day. This is the perfect time to brush up on water safety.

Water Safety Tips

❀ Learn how to swim yourself.

❀ Enroll your children in swimming classes.

❀ Supervise children closely, even with a lifeguard present.

❀ Don't depend on floats; they can drift off.

❀ Avoid diving head first unless water depth has been determined carefully.

❀ Be vigilant about locking pool gates.

❀ Contact the Red Cross or YMCA for lifeguard and water-safety classes and tips.

❀ Familiarize yourself with local water conditions at lakes and/or beaches before swimming.

❀ Don't forget the sunscreen!

A Smoke Arose From the Land

The sun and sky were darkened by the smoke from the Abyss (Revelation 9:2).

J.R.R. Tolkien, in his book *The Two Towers,* tells the story of Isengard, a city ruled by a fallen wizard. The dark tower at the center of the city pours forth smoke day and night as it tirelessly churns out an arsenal of weapons. The surrounding land is laid waste. The forests are decimated to feed the forges. The mountain streams are dammed and diverted to run the machinery. Dark clouds of smoke block out the sun. Waste water flows out of the tower, poisoning the streams. The fish die, the animals grow sick.

Tolkien and C. S. Lewis spent hours trekking the Welsh countryside together. I can imagine Tolkien's growing distress as he watched the countryside gouged by the effects of spreading industrialization. His outrage found expression in his writing. In his parable, the trees themselves awake and march on Isengard. They destroy the dam, flood the forges, and dismantle the town stone by stone, leaving only the ruined and now silent tower. The land is swept clean. What of today? How is our land to be swept clean of smog, industrial pollution, and toxic waste? Is there any hope of renewal?

THOUGHTS TO PONDER

❀ Because I believe in the Second Advent, does that give me permission to ignore environmental concerns?

❀ What can I personally do to protect the natural resources God has blessed us with?

"In nature there are neither rewards nor punishments—there are consequences."
—Robert Ingersoll

FRUIT SKEWERS WITH YOGURT SAUCE
SEASONAL PRODUCE

Pay a visit to your local farmer's market and enjoy the sights and smells of the season. Select whatever fresh fruit strikes your fancy. The following list is just a suggestion. Fruit kabobs make a dramatic presentation as appetizers, salad, or dessert but are easy enough for kids to assemble. They carry well for potluck or a picnic. Preparation time: 20 minutes. Serves 12-24.

Pantry Items
24 wooden kabob skewers

Fresh Items
Fresh fruit in season
    Cantelope
    Watermellon
    Strawberries
    Grapes
    Peaches
Fresh mint (2 sprigs)
Lemon (1)
Large carton of vanilla yogurt

DIRECTIONS
Wash, peel, and cut fruit into 1-inch cubes. Thread fruit on wooden skewers. Squeeze fresh lemon on fruit to avoid discoloration. Rinse and pat dry mint sprigs. Dice one sprig of mint very fine and mix into yogurt. Store fruit and yogurt in separate airtight containers in refrigerator until ready to serve. To serve, arrange fruit skewers on a platter. Pour yogurt into a small serving bowl and garnish with reserved mint sprig.

Babylon Is Fallen

Babylon has fallen, has fallen! All the images of its gods lie shattered on the ground! (Isaiah 21:9).

Babylon towers over prophecy, much as the postdiluvian tower towered over the Plain of Shinar and as Nebuchadnezzar's golden image towered over the Babylonian Empire. Babylon is the symbol of human hubris, the coronation of the self-made god. We can make it on our own. We can determine our own destiny. We can build towers to the sky and soar into the heavens. We can pierce the heart of an atom. We can create life in a laboratory. Are we not as gods? Are we not wise and powerful and increased with knowledge? We have no need of God save for our dark hearts. Who will heal the black hearts of men and women? As the tower falls and the atom explodes, "all the images of its gods lie shattered on the ground." Our hearts cry out to God, our Father. Like children, we cry Abba!

THOUGHTS TO PONDER

❀ Insulated by technology, affluence, and independence, do I sometimes lose sight of God?

❀ Are life crises the only times I yearn to understand the will of God for my life?

"There is hardly a man clever enough to recognize the full extent of the evil he does."
—*Francois de La Rochefoucauld*

"PLEIN-AIR" WATERCOLOR PAINTING
SUNNY DAY ACTIVITY

Ages: Grade School to Adult
Materials Needed:
    Pencils
    Watercolor paint (any type)
    Brushes (assorted sizes)
    Watercolor paper (pad or single sheets)
    Clean sponges
    Old toothbrush

Plein-Air is a fancy term for painting outdoors and observing outdoor light. Even if the paintings are very abstract and impressionistic, your children (as well as you) will have a great time. Stress that art doesn't have to be an exact copy. Following are a few simple guidelines to keep it fun:

- Use the three-line rule to pencil in the under drawing. (Yes, it can be five lines, but it helps to keep the under drawing simple and not too detailed.) Example: a line for the horizon, a jagged line for foreground trees, a curving line for a lake or path.
- Lightly wet one section of the drawing. Load a brush with paint and touch it to the wet part of the paper. Watch the paint spread across the wet area. Move the paint around or let the paint "run wild." Try adding another color to the opposite side of the wet area and watch the colors blend. Dry in the sun before starting the next area.
- When painting is dry, dab a piece of torn sponge in paint to add foliage or rock textures. Rub an old toothbrush in paint and flick it on the painting to add flower flecks or insects.
- Stay open to whatever develops. Experiment using twigs and grass as brushes. Enjoy! You will "see" your surroundings with a brand-new "eye" as your painting unfolds.

All Things Made New

Some days this earth seems very dark and ugly. Violated by sin and wanton destruction, careless pollution, and the mindless stripping of its natural resources, the land is burned, the rivers run with wormwood, the sea creatures die, and the sky is dark with smog. God's magnificent creation is stripped and desecrated by human greed and carelessness. Some days I grieve for what we have done and what we cannot undo. But as Christians, we are not left without hope. We know that one fine day, we will stand by the shoulder of God and watch a world unfurl at the sound of His voice. I can't imagine a price not worth paying for that incredible sound-and-light extravaganza. Of course, the price has already been paid. Our ticket has already been purchased. You and I have a backstage pass to the rebirth of the universe, courtesy of the Creative Director! *Even so come, Lord Jesus, Amen!*

THOUGHTS TO PONDER

❀ Adam and Eve were appointed "caretakers" in Eden. What does that mean to Christians today?

❀ What will that mean in the earth made new?

"I saw a new heaven and a new earth, for the first heaven and the first earth had passed away."
"He who was seated on the throne said, 'I am making everything new!' "—John the revelator

BEAUTIFUL STORAGE SPACES

We may not be able to solve world pollution this week, but we can tidy up our little corner of the universe. Cleaning cluttered spaces refreshes our sense of well-being. Few things make a woman feel more satisfied and in control of her life than organizing a closet or cupboard. Whoever said, "A place for everything and everything in its place," knew all there is to know about keeping things tidy. Why not pick a storage area or workspace this weekend that has been neglected for way too long and give it a makeover?

❋ **Storage Containers**. If things are out of place, it usually means that we don't have a place to put them or it is too difficult to put them there. What does your storage space need—see-through containers, easy-open or lidless containers, easy-to-read labels? I bet your favorite home-supply store has all those things. Or you could recycle glass jars, shoeboxes, cans with lids, and oatmeal boxes with pretty adhesive paper and sticky labels.

❋ **Hooks and Clips**. Hooks and wall clips are much easier to install than shelving. Take a good look at your storage space. Perhaps all you need is a few well-placed hooks. Home-supply and container stores have a wonderful variety of hooks and clips, ranging from teacup size to industrial strength. Unwieldy items such as rakes, brooms, and shovels behave beautifully when corralled on a wall rack.

❋ **Shelving.** I consider new shelving a last resort. If you are installing shelves yourself, be prepared to spend plenty of time measuring and securing correctly, or your shelves will surely come tumbling down. If you're a handywoman, this may be the perfect option for you. However, if you're like me, consider ready-made or stackable shelves. They may be a little more pricey than installing shelves yourself, but certainly more convenient.

❋ **Donation Box.** Finally, if you don't need it, don't keep it. Storing unused items doesn't make good sense unless you have endless storage capacity at your disposal. If you're not using an item, perhaps someone else might be able to. When clearing out cluttered spaces, set aside the donation box before you start. It's a good thing.

Let My Heart Sing

Indeed, to them you are nothing more than one who sings loves songs with a beautiful voice and plays an instrument well, for they hear your words but do not put them into practice (Ezekiel 33:32).

What's your favorite love song? Is it about love's longing or love's loss? Is it sweet or bittersweet? Love songs are so personal, so intimate. Love songs pin our memories to the timeline of our life. A great love song can awaken a smoldering romance; it can carry us through the hard times. A great love song helps us remember when we needed nothing but each other. Of course, a great love song can also be ruined by a badly ended love affair, forever turning the sweet notes sour to our ears. Long after the relationship is ended and the song is no longer "ours," we still feel cheated and manipulated whenever the refrain intrudes uninvited on our busy lives. Who would have thought God feels the same way about love songs?

THOUGHTS TO PONDER
- ❀ Is there a special song or hymn that makes me feel particularly close to God?
- ❀ Am I sometimes guilty of singing hymns to God with just my voice and not my heart?

"To try to write love is to confront the muck of language: that region of hysteria where language is both too much and too little, excessive and impoverished."—Roland Barthes, 1915-1980

OUR SONG

Think back to a particularly romantic and special time in your courtship or marriage. Remembering those times together is a wonderful way to keep love alive and flourishing. Do you have a special song, a favorite restaurant, a romantic vacation, or a special place? Finding ways to connect, little reminders of what makes us special, keeps the love light in our eyes on even the busiest weeks. Consider some ways you can trigger pleasant memories. Here are a few ideas that won't take a lot of time or planning but are sure to reap big dividends:

❀ Slip an old love letter into his briefcase. Imagine his surprise and delight when he finds it.
❀ Snuggle up after the kids are in bed tonight with a photo album of a special vacation the two of you shared.
❀ Find a CD version of your special song and leave it on his car seat.
❀ Rent a video or DVD of the first movie you saw together, pop some popcorn, and dim the lights.

Sometimes we temporarily forget how special our loved ones are. A few gentle breaths can keep the fires smoldering.

Rejoice in the Lord Always

This is the day the LORD has made; let us rejoice and be glad in it (Psalm 118:24).

What is it that keeps us from rejoicing always? Is it that our bosses are too demanding; our husbands are too insensitive; our kids are too disrespectful; our parents are too critical; our church is too cold; our house is too small; our friends are too busy; our thighs are too flabby? Or is it that we overlook the tiny gifts God wraps up just for us each day? In our rush to get the kids fed, we may have failed to notice how plump and delicious the blueberries were this morning. We may have been too harried to see the awesome sky show God put on during our drive to work. Perhaps we were even too preoccupied with the day's agenda to enjoy a couple of hugs with the cutest kids in the world before shooing them out the door. When we finally made it into bed last night, did we pause to offer a silent prayer of thanks for the man who faithfully shares our bed night after night after night (even if he does snore)? Life without blueberries and sunrises and friends and family to love might be hard. And some of us certainly have it hard, but so many of us have it so good! It's a mystery why we don't rejoice in the Lord always!

THOUGHTS TO PONDER

❀ What blessings from God might I be missing because I stay too busy to notice?

❀ Is it possible in this day and age to teach my children to live life with gratitude?

"Gratitude is the inward feeling of kindness received. Thankfulness is the natural impulse to express that feeling. Thanksgiving is the following of that impulse."—Henry Van Dyke, American Protestant clergyman and writer, 1852–1933

GIFT DIARY

Gift shops usually carry a selection of beautiful bound books for brides and expectant mothers to use to record their shower gifts. Wouldn't it be great to keep a gift diary of the wonderful blessings and answers to prayer that God showers us with every day? Keep a personal gift diary for a month, or share one with your family. You can purchase one from a gift shop, or you can make your own. Either way, your gift diary should be very special and include daily entries. If you decide to make your own, here are a few ideas to get you going:

1. Ask your kids to help you cover an everyday notebook with a collage of cut out magazine pictures representing some of our everyday blessings.
2. Purchase a scrapbook and spend Friday evening or Sabbath afternoon decorating the entries with cutouts, drawings, and/or pictures.
3. Tape a large calendar page to the fridge. Invite family members to pencil in their "God gifts" for the week. Review it together for Friday sundown worship.
4. Place a "gift box" by the phone with a notepad and pen. Encourage family members to jot down a blessing and slip it into the "gift box." Empty the box together once a week for family worship.

Clap Your Hands

Clap your hands, all you nations; shout to God with cries of joy. How awesome is the LORD Most High, the great King over all the earth! (Psalm 47:1, 2).

We clap enthusiastically at school plays, band concerts, and basketball games. But we're often a little confused about when to clap in church. Some churches do. Some churches don't, and some churches can't quite make up their minds about whether they do or they don't.

Can you remember the last time you clapped and squealed for joy? Was it when you got your first two-wheeler with the tassels on the handles and the flowers on the spokes? It was probably just before you officially became a "young woman," whenever it was that that portentous date arrived. Our responses are a little more ladylike these days. It's not appropriate to erupt with whooping and wild clapping at our age, is it? But have you stood on a mountain and watched as the wind swept down across the valley and the grasses writhed and danced in the sun? Did you wish you could join in? Have you felt the pull in your soul to spread your arms and spin with joy? "How awesome is the LORD Most High, the great King over all the earth!" I have no idea whether I can still do cartwheels, but some days I wonder. I'd like to think I still could if I really wanted to.

THOUGHTS TO PONDER

❀ Am I sometimes afraid to express joy? What am I afraid of?

❀ How would it affect my life if I responded more openly to joyful feelings?

"He has spent his life best who has enjoyed it most. God will take care that we do not enjoy it any more than is good for us."—Samuel Butler, British poet, satirist, 1612-1680

BODY MOVEMENT

If you grew up like I did, you're probably a little cautious about body movement. Sometimes we realize too late that we have a body, that it was made primarily to move, and that we're not moving it half as much as we should. Exercise, if we can find the time for it, seems like such a serious chore. How did that happen? When we were kids, we couldn't stop moving. We did it just for the fun of it. We still can! Here are a few silly ideas from a "closet kid." Try it in the privacy of your basement, in the backyard, in the dark, or in the living room when nobody is home. You can laugh if you want to; there's nobody around to watch. If your kids catch you acting silly, I have to warn you, they will laugh their little butts off, but they'll want to join you.

1. Tie a long ribbon to the end of a pencil and dance to the *Nutcracker Suite.* Leap and spin, but keep the ribbon from touching the floor! For a real workout, try two ribbons.
2. Turn on the kids' *Silly Songs* tape. Can you still skip and jump rope to "Mabel, Mabel, set the table"? Yeah!
3. Put a good gospel choir on the sound system and crank up the volume. Sing and shout and clap those hands! Big movements, high above your head for terrific aerobics. Can you say, "Amen, Sister"?
4. Marching bands and show tunes are an almost irresistible invitation to act like a kid. Step high and look alive, soldier! If you'd like to feel a little younger, try acting like a kid for fifteen or twenty minutes every day!

With Shouts of Joy

Sing to the Lord a new song. . . . Let them shout from the mountaintops (Isaiah 42:10, 11).

Shouting exudes power. The walls of Jericho descended after a shout. Gideon's ragtag band routed the Midianite army with a mighty shout. Shouts of joy can charge large crowds with electrifying power. We've all experienced that emotional surge at ball games, inaugurations, and concerts. But why would God want us to shout? What occasion would prompt godly shouts of joy? It seems a little improper to shout, doesn't it? I mean, we wouldn't want to shout in church; that would be irreverent. I have a lot of difficulty imagining shouting with joy in most of the churches I've been in. So where should the people shout? Could we shout from a mountaintop, as Isaiah suggests? Could we shout in a forest? Riddle: If a woman shouts alone in a forest and nobody hears, is she really shouting? I have no answer to this question, but I fear if we continue to refuse to shout, the rocks will cry out.

THOUGHTS TO PONDER

❀ What message are my actions shouting to my coworkers and family?

❀ What if I have nothing to say?

"For twenty-five centuries, Western knowledge has tried to look upon the world. It has failed to understand that the world is not for the beholding. It is for hearing. It is not legible, but audible. Our science has always desired to monitor, measure, abstract, and castrate meaning, forgetting that life is full of noise and that death alone is silent: work noise, noise of man, and noise of beast. Noise bought, sold, or prohibited. Nothing essential happens in the absence of noise."
—Jacques Attali, Algerian-born French economist, writer, 1943-

PUBLIC SPEAKING

Fear of public speaking is one of the greatest fears of American adults. Bad memories from botched childhood performances can dog us for the rest of our lives, rendering otherwise competent adults into stammering idiots when forced to stand in front of an audience of our peers. Apparently the only good news is that just about everybody else is in the same boat we are. But it is not hopeless. Some people do overcome their fear, and there are things we can do to minimize our discomfort and improve our public performances. Try some stage actor's advice:

1. **Prepare, prepare, prepare.** Contrary to popular myth, you can't over-prepare for a presentation. But if you think you can wing it, you will probably regret it.
2. **Rehearse, rehearse, rehearse.** Even if you plan to read your speech word for word, you need to run through it a couple of times before you actually deliver it. If you're presenting from notes, plan on practicing out loud at least once for every five minutes your speech is supposed to last.
3. **Sing and Shout.** No kidding! The best way to avoid the dreaded deadpan delivery is to practice singing or shouting your presentation. It loosens up your vocal chords, as well as your inhibitions.
4. **Visualize Success.** Your subconscious will do whatever you tell it to. If you obsess on visions of humiliation, your body will undoubtedly obey. Stay focused on images of your delivering a dynamic, well-accepted presentation.
5. **Break a leg, kiddo!**

Dancing Before the Lord

We dance at weddings and baptisms—but not in church. Excuse me? You didn't know we danced at baptisms? Well, we do! As a matter of fact, our General Conference president dances at baptisms. I once saw him leading a procession of brightly dressed Yorba women in matching dresses and turbans right through the center of town. Or rather, to be more accurate, they were leading him. This tall, fair-haired man caught up in a joyful melee. The women were singing, clapping, and dancing to the rhythm of drums as they escorted the newly converted villagers the half mile to the river. It would have been impossible not to join in. I'm happy to report that our General Conference president is not impossible. I'm happy to report that this man of God knows a thing or two about joy.

THOUGHT TO PONDER

❀ Has my relationship with God included joyful responses to His grace?

"You turned my wailing into dancing; you removed my sackcloth and clothed me with joy, that my heart may sing to you and not be silent. O LORD my God, I will give you thanks forever."
—The Psalmist

NO-COOK LASAGNA
FAST & EASY PREP

This easy lasagna casserole does not require precooking the noodles. By using fresh veggies and cottage cheese in place of traditional meat and ricotta cheese, the dry noodles cook by absorbing the extra moisture. Preparation time: 20 minutes. Baking time: approximately 60 minutes. Rest 10 minutes after removing from oven.

Pantry Items
Lasagna noodles (1 box)
Spaghetti sauce (1 jar)
Salt (1 tsp.)

Fresh Items
Cottage cheese (1 carton)
Fresh veggies (4 cups, thinly sliced)
Parmesan cheese (2 cups)
Shredded mozzarella cheese (4 cups)
Fresh oregano (2 Tbsp., chopped)
Garlic (1 clove, minced)

DIRECTIONS
Preheat oven to 350° F. Thinly slice 4 cups of fresh veggies, such as sweet onions, fresh mushrooms, spinach, bell peppers, or zucchini, depending on what your family likes and what you may have fresh from the garden. Set aside veggies. In a medium bowl, combine cottage cheese, 1 cup Parmesan cheese, chopped oregano, and minced garlic. Cover the bottom of a 9" x 12" baking casserole with 1/2 of the spaghetti sauce. Lay one layer of lasagna noodles on top of the sauce. Break dry noodles to fit spaces so casserole bottom is covered evenly with lasagna noodles. Spread 1/2 of the cottage cheese mixture on top of the dry lasagna. Layer 1/2 of the sliced veggies evenly over the cottage cheese and sprinkle with 1/2 tsp. salt, 1/3 cup Parmesan cheese, and 1 cup mozarella cheese. Drizzle 1/4 of spaghetti sauce over cheese. Repeat layer. Cover top layer of dry lasagna noodles with remaining spaghetti sauce. Cover with foil and bake for 40 minutes, remove foil, sprinkle casserole with remaining mozzarella and Parmesan cheese, and return to oven. Lasagna is finished when fork inserted in center easily pierces noodles and sauce is bubbling in the center. Remove lasagna from oven and let rest at least 10 to 15 minutes before serving.

Year of Jubilee

For six years you are to sow your fields and harvest the crops, but during the seventh year let the land lie unplowed and unused (Exodus 23:10).

An entire year dedicated to joy and celebration. What was God thinking? He issues an order to Israel—every seven years the work stops and the country parties! And every fifty years the poverty-stricken get their property back. I thought God was a capitalist, didn't you? I mean, what happened to the good old work ethic as in "go to the ant thou sluggard"?

Apparently God also believes in "go to the party, thou dreadful bore." Ever since Adam and Eve managed to get kicked out of Eden, life on this earth has been hard. We work hard to survive; we labor to give birth; we slave to make ends meet. We forget we were created for God's pleasure, not in a fit of sadistic irony as some sober Christians might lead you to believe. Sin turns everything on its ear. The good are deadly serious; the bad are party goers. Shouldn't it be the other way around?

THOUGHT TO PONDER

❋ Sometimes when I'm watching toddlers play "grown-up" with grave seriousness, I have to smile. Do you suppose God ever smiles the same way when He watches us seriously playing "Christian"?

" 'Except ye become as little children,' except you can wake on your fiftieth birthday with the same forward-looking excitement and interest in life that you enjoyed when you were five, 'ye cannot enter the kingdom of God.' One must not only die daily, but every day we must be born again."—Dorothy L. Sayers, British author, 1893-1957

TRAVEL POSTER FOR HEAVEN
INSIDE ACTIVITY

Ages: 5 to 12
Materials Needed:
> A poster board for each child (select light colors)
> Poster paints
> Assorted stickers (animals, birds, angels, Jesus, flowers, etc.)
> Glitter and glue (optional)

The object is to create a travel poster of heaven by painting in a simple background and then adding stickers to complete the landscape. Adding glitter just makes it extra special!

DIRECTIONS
Help the children decide whether they want their posters to stand up and down (vertical) or sideways (horizontal). Next, help them draw in a horizon line (it doesn't have to be exactly straight) about 1/3 of the way down from the top. The area above the horizon is sky. The area below is land. They can paint clouds or rainbows in the sky. Trees, buildings, and lakes can be painted below the horizon line. When the paint dries, start adding stickers. When they have completed their composition, you may want to help them outline parts of their painting in glitter. Outline an object (such as a rainbow or the Holy City) by squeezing out a thin strip of white glue. Sprinkle with glitter and allow it to dry. They will be very proud of their heaven poster. Now you'll have to find a place to hang it!

Strike the Tambourine

Little girls love tambourines! Especially pretty tambourines with shiny bells and colorful ribbons. If you've ever watched a little girl with a tambourine, you can't help but notice how she loses herself in the moment; music, ribbon, movement, noise, and laughter flow through her, in her, and around her. It is joy, just joy, only joy. She is not worried about making too much noise, looking silly, or feeling foolish. She is interested only in the tambourine and making it dance for her.

As we grow older, we look for other amusements to lose ourselves in. From makeup, to boys, to homes of our own, we are fascinated with pretty things that make us forget our dreadful self-consciousness. We desperately want to feel beautiful, happy, and graceful instead of plain, awkward, and alone. What would happen if we picked up a pretty tambourine with shiny bells and colorful ribbons and danced?

I will build you up again and you will be rebuilt, O Virgin Israel. Again you will take up your tambourines and go out to dance with the joyful (Jeremiah 31:4).

THOUGHTS TO PONDER

❀ What makes me feel happy and beautiful?

❀ Is there any reason why I shouldn't make time to do that today?

"You must understand the whole of life, not just one little part of it. That is why you must read, that is why you must look at the skies, that is why you must sing, and dance, and write poems, and suffer, and understand; for all that is life."
—Jiddu Krishnamurti, Indian philosopher, 1895-1986

BEAUTIFUL EXPRESSIONS

We get so busy meeting the needs of our family and community that we often postpone attending to our own needs. Eventually it catches up with us. Stress, eating disorders, soft addictions, poor health, anxiety—these results of self-neglect can send us spiraling into depression and despair. If we don't exercise judicious self-care, we eventually cannot take care of anyone else either. It's a pay-me-now or pay-me-later game. Life won't stop if you take a little time out to pamper yourself. Pick one or two of the self-care activities listed below or come up with some of your own. Engage in something that will help you feel refreshed and beautiful this week. Your whole family will be glad you did.

Make an appointment for:
A massage
A pedicure
A manicure
A facial
A makeover
A new hairstyle

Go on a shopping trip alone to purchase something just for you:
Flowers
Perfume
Cosmetics
Intimate apparel
Candles
Accessories

Set aside some private time to:
Take a long bath
Read a book
Take a walk
Play an instrument
Enjoy a hobby
Take a drive with your favorite CDs

Happy Birthday

Happy Birthday to you! You are so very important, not just to your family but to hundreds of people you haven't even met yet. God has fashioned you with great care and hopes. He has held up time so you could become one of His precious daughters. Of course, what you're doing right now is important. If it were not for you, the universe would be void of some of its brightest lights, but what you're doing right now on this earth is really only a prelude. Your real job will probably be clear to you some five million years from now. You were created for eternity. You were created to play a role that transcends the few short years you will spend on this planet. You were created as unique as fingerprints, snowflakes, and DNA. Don't ever kid yourself into thinking that you are anything less than extraordinary. You're not. What you are and what you will become will resonate through the halls of time. Be kind to yourself. Take care of yourself. I am sure that someplace, sometime, we will become great friends, and I will thank you personally for allowing God's love to flow through you. Happy Birthday to you, I am so glad you were born!

THOUGHTS TO PONDER

❊ Have I ever stopped to consider how short my time on this earth will seem?

❊ How does it make me feel to know that God not only has a part for me to play right here, right now, but throughout eternity as well?

"I believe love produces a certain flowering of the whole personality which nothing else can achieve."—Ivan Sergeevich

MENTORS

A recent study identified the single most important factor in helping impoverished children build successful adult lives. That factor was having an adult who took an interest in them. The child could make it with the help of only one involved adult, and that adult didn't even have to be a parent. It could be a teacher, a minister, a grandparent. One involved adult—and a kid received a chance at success! That study shows us again that mentoring is a sacred obligation. Mentoring can make all the difference in the world. If we accomplish anything in life, it is because somewhere along the way someone has helped us. In the circle of life, our best thanks can be to mentor someone in return. Do we know someone who could benefit from our involved interest?

❀ A single mother
❀ A teenager at church
❀ A foster child
❀ A coworker
❀ A neighborhood child
❀ A college student
❀ A kid in church school

Groups that need and welcome mentors:
❀ Pathfinders
❀ Church schools
❀ Big Sisters
❀ Women's organizations
❀ Small business associations
❀ Community service organizations

Gift Exchange

Do you love gifts? Not only those pretty gifts your sister gives you wrapped in hand-printed parchment paper and tied with an organza ribbon. Pencil holders wrapped in crayoned butcher paper and heart-shaped pins still in the discount-store bag—do you love those too? There is something so spirit-lifting about receiving a gift. I think we're all suckers for gifts. Which gifts make your list of top-ten gifts of all time? Mine includes a pewter belt buckle from my kid brother, left unwrapped in my college mailbox after a weekend visit, a puppy, a poem, a trash bag full of trinkets, a crayon-marker portrait, and a potted violet from my eleven-year-old son. The list could go on, but the thread that weaves through each memory is the unexpectedness of the gift, the total surprise, the complete lack of occasion. It feels like love.

Sometimes I wonder how God feels about the gifts He so lavishly bestows upon us day after day, year after year. I wonder whether it bothers Him that we don't notice. I wonder how many more gifts our loving heavenly Father is waiting to pour out if we would just be willing to accept them?

If you, then, though you are evil, know how to give good gifts to your children, how much more will your Father in heaven give good gifts to those who ask him! (Matthew 7:11).

THOUGHTS TO PONDER

❀ Who in your life deserves a surprise gift?

❀ Am I open to receiving God's gifts with delight today?

"Only when your consciousness is totally focused on the moment you are in can you receive whatever gift, lesson, or delight that moment has to offer."
—Barbara de Angelis, American author

SURPRISE GIFTS

Children are inherently generous. They love selecting, making, and giving gifts. As adults, it is easy to forget how frustrating it is for children when it comes to gift giving. They can't just hop into a car and go purchase a gift. Help your children select a recipient for a surprise gift this week and allow them to do some chores for you to earn the money to purchase the gift. Make a date to take them shopping to the store of their choice. You will have a wonderful time, they will have a wonderful time, and you will make one very surprised individual happy! What could be better than that?

Life of the Party

Do you know someone who is always the life of the party? There is something about a party that is always a little out of control. Those of us who cherish control and predictability are sometimes put off by parties. We prefer scripted events where everybody's lines are well rehearsed. I have to admit that I can sympathize with Michal, David's first wife. She had been brought up as princess in her father's court. Saul had a lot of problems, but apparently a kingly manner was one of his major assets. I can imagine little Princess Michal solemnly following her regal father around the court. Then the great warrior David sweeps into town, and the women break out in droves to welcome him. David has eyes only for the Princess Michal. No wonder she falls for him so hard. This is the stuff fairytales are made of.

Unfortunately, all did not end well. Her handsome, young husband is soon exiled from court. Her father marries her off to another nobleman, and by the time David gets around to sending for her, years have passed, and he has acquired a harem of wives. Michal's ex-husband follows her caravan all the way to Jerusalem, weeping. He may not have been able to bestow the title of queen upon her, but he certainly knew how to treat her like one. Michal watches from her balcony as the ark of the covenant is transported into the capital, Jerusalem. David has declared a national holiday! Always at home in a crowd, David is in his element. The ark is finally coming home! It is what he has spent the last twenty years hoping for. "God with us" at last! David is leading a procession of dancing women. As the day becomes hotter, and the festivity continues, the dancing king sheds his kingly robes one by one as Michal looks on in horror. Finally, David is clothed only in his loincloth, leaping and dancing with all his might in a very, how shall we put it, common manner. Of course, a woman of Michal's sensibilities would be offended. When the ark is finally installed with full ceremony, David returns to the royal palace and Michal's biting sarcasm. Both biblical accounts of this little domestic spat concur that, by this time, Michal is not merely embarrassed or uncomfortable, she is furious. She despises David. She has just witnessed what she considers his total lack of refinement, and she completely missed the remarkable passion of a man after God's own heart. A cautionary tale for all us women of "refined sensibilities." (See 1 Samuel 18:20–19:17; 25:42-44; 2 Samuel 3:13-16; 6:12-23.)

THOUGHTS TO PONDER

❀ Am I ever offended by expressions of joy?
❀ Do I believe God approves more of discrete expressions of joy than passionate expressions?

"Possibly, more people kill themselves and others out of hurt vanity than out of envy, jealousy, malice or desire for revenge."— Iris Murdoch, British novelist, 1919-1999

MY GUY

He's our hero, our knight in shining armor, the love of our lives. So what if he's not perfect; neither are we. We could pick and nag and enumerate his many shortcomings, but it won't make our home a kinder, gentler place for anybody. And unfortunately, he could probably come up with his own list. Why not make a list of our guy's best qualities and stick it in his pocket? Remember, longer is better, and no backhanded compliments, just the real deal. After all, you've got great taste; you picked him. Bet he'd like to know why, again!

Life Is Beautiful

In the 1998 Grand Prix winning film *Life Is Beautiful,* by Roberto Benigni, a loving family overwhelmed by Nazi terrorism is sustained by the irrepressible will of the protagonist, Guido. Guido is determined to preserve his young son's childlike innocence. Guido's comic humor takes on heroic proportions as he turns internment in a Nazi concentration camp into an imaginary game. Through sheer force of will and wit, Guido provides a happy childhood for his son in the worst possible circumstances.

Our children are so precious to us. We deeply desire that their childhood should be innocent of the real terrors of this world. Goodness always protects, always nurtures. Evil always destroys, always disrupts. It is the great controversy. Nazis were evil on a grand scale. But evil can come in small, petty packages too. What family hasn't experienced the tyranny of a selfish and manipulative member who turns every family gathering into a dismal assault on joy? What congregation lacks a bitter and toxic member bent on hurtful, self-serving gossip? The sacred joy of life can be assaulted on many fronts. But life is and remains beautiful. Life is a gift. Aren't we obligated to cherish it? Don't our children deserve protection from even petty terrorism? Every day that we are able to share God's joy and blessings with our children, we strike a blow against evil. We give them the priceless gift of joy. Life is beautiful—for at least one more day.

THOUGHTS TO PONDER

❀ Is my life expressed in protective and nurturing actions or in destructive and disruptive actions?

❀ How can I help my children enjoy life even in the midst of difficult circumstances?

> *"To cultivate the sense of the beautiful, is one of the most effectual ways of cultivating an appreciation of the divine goodness."—St. Pierre*

MEMORY BOOKS

Scrapbooking has become very popular again! Any craft store you visit will probably have an entire section devoted to special papers, cutouts, stickers, and preprinted borders for a scrapbook project. If you aren't already creating memory books, you might consider experimenting with scrapbooking, a hobby both you and your kids can enjoy together. The fun part is creating the memories. Following are two summer adventure ideas you can enjoy with your kids and then enjoy again and again by turning the mementos into a scrapbook. I bet your family can think of several more.

- ❀ **Bus Adventure.** If you live near public transportation, a surprise bus adventure can be a lot of fun. Take a bus to a museum, park, or library. Or just see where the bus takes you! Find a local hangout for lunch. Snap lots of pictures, collect napkins, brochures, and postcards for your memory book. The important thing is the time you spend and the memories you share together.
- ❀ **Family Vacation.** Give each child a disposable camera and let them record the trip from their point of view. Encourage them to find a free souvenir at each place you stop. After the film is developed, let your kids write their memories beside their pictures in the memory book. If you have a blended family, this is a wonderful exercise to develop and record bonding memories together.

Pretty Packages

We all love pretty packages, don't we? I admire a woman who knows how to tie a bow! (There's a skill that can take years to master.) Does it ever strike you as a little silly to spend so much time and attention on the wrapping when we all know it's the gift that counts? If you received a string of pearls, would you really care what the package looked like? Well, of course, you would!

Even the Bible assumes we all know that a pigsty is not a proper setting for pearls. When we stop to consider how exquisitely God has packaged His greatest gift, life, we might be a little more careful about how we tie our bows. Life comes wrapped in a rainbow of colors, a bouquet of scents, a full palate of flavors, a dazzling array of sensory touch, and a symphony of sounds. Life has been exquisitely gift wrapped for us. Even marred by sin, even in its fallen, sinful state, earth abounds with pretty packages for us to unwrap. I have to believe it is because God delights to delight us.

THOUGHTS TO PONDER

❀ Have I ever considered "wrapping" the everyday gifts I give to my family in a special way?

❀ How can I make my daily activities an expression of love, not of drudgery?

TABOULI
SEASONAL PRODUCE

This is a great summer salad made with fresh veggies from the garden or farmer's market! Presoak bulgur and wheat berries: 2 to 3 hours. (Wheat berries are raw wheat grains.) Preparation time: 20 minutes. Serves 8

Pantry Items
Wheat bulgur (1 cup)
Wheat berries (1 cup)
Olive oil (3/4 cup)
Salt and pepper (1 tsp. or to taste)
Allspice (1 tsp.)
*Pita Bread (4 flat loaves)

Fresh Items
Parsley (4 cups, minced)
Cucumber (1)
Mint (1 cup, minced)
Tomatoes (4)
Red onion (1)
Garlic (1 clove)
Lemon (1)
*Lettuce (8 medium leaves)

*Optional item: see serving suggestions

DIRECTIONS
Soak bulgur and wheat berries in cold water in separate covered bowls for 2 to 3 hours. Rinse and drain bulgur. Boil wheat berries briefly until just tender, rinse in cold water, and drain. Mince parsley, mint, and garlic. Dice cucumber, tomatoes, and onion. Combine vegetables and herbs with bulgur and wheat berries in a large bowl. Squeeze juice from lemon and combine with olive oil, salt, pepper, and allspice in a small bowl. Whisk well and drizzle over bulgur. Toss to mix well. Cover and refrigerate 4 hours or overnight.

SERVING SUGGESTIONS
- Divide and scoop tabouli salad unto 12 lettuce leaves and place on platter. Cut flat loaves in half and serve beside tabouli.
- Stuff pita bread with tabouli and lettuce for a great sandwich.

He Played for Us the Pipe

You may have seen her at church. She is the one who is always there, helping out with potluck, collecting the Sabbath School attendance charts, faithfully attending board meetings. She is nothing if she is not faithful! If you try to thank her for all her hard work, she will probably demur, saying something like, "Just trying to help out the best I can." Undoubtedly the members of her church depend on her too much. They take advantage of her responsible character. No sooner is one burden laid down, but she immediately snatches up another with a wicked glance over her shoulder at Mary, hanging about the guest speaker while the dishes pile up! Christ starts humming a nursery rhyme; the children chant, "We played for you the pipe, but you would not dance." Would it occur to Martha, in the midst of all her good works, that the Master might like to see her dance? Perhaps it would please Him to see her let go, relax, and enjoy herself. No. I don't think that would ever occur to Martha.

THOUGHTS TO PONDER

❊ Does Martha's attitude sometimes sneak up on me and stare at me from the mirror?

❊ How many good things do I miss because I stay too busy to enjoy them?

"Few things are harder to put up with than a good example."—Mark Twain

ROCK/SHELL COLLECTION
OUTSIDE ACTIVITY

Ages: 6 to Adult
Materials Needed:
> Field guide on shells/rocks (available at nature stores, bookstores, and some park stores)
> Sturdy net bag or bucket for collecting

Optional Materials:
> Wood panel 1/2" thick (large enough to display collection)
> 2 screw eyes and picture wire
> Glue gun
> Sticky labels

This is a great activity to start during a camping trip or vacation to the beach. The object is to collect as many different types of rocks or shells as possible and then to try to identify them with the field guide. It appeals to the treasure hunter in all of us. Kids of all ages throw a lot of energy into this project.

When you get home, you may enjoy working together to display your collection. Find or purchase a wooden panel at least 1/2-inch thick, large enough to accommodate the collection. Arrange the rocks or shells on the board, leaving space for the labels. With the assistance of an adult, use the glue gun to attach the rocks or shells to the board. (Obviously, very large specimens will not work.) Print or handwrite the names on the specimens on the labels to identify each rock or shell. Insert the screw eyes on the back of the panel and run a double length of picture wire through the screw eyes so the collection can be hung on a wall. In addition to being a great learning experience, the display will be a wonderful family memento for years to come.

I Come to the Garden

Do you find gardens irresistible? Beautiful, romantic, intimate—gardens revive wilting spirits the way the morning dew revives roses. God carved out a garden home in Eden for the beautiful young couple He had just created. Can you imagine what God's garden would look like? What would it smell like? Close your eyes for a moment and imagine the garden God might create special, just for you. Would it have the sound of water trickling through it? Would the air be filled with delicate floral scents? Would there be a riot of blossoms or deep-green fern banks? Would your garden have a wild, romantic look like a hidden meadow? Or would it be exquisitely tended with beds of exotic blooms? What kind of garden would God design, just for you and Him to visit in at the end of each day? I think one of the saddest, most poignant verses in the Bible begins, "Then the man and his wife heard the sound of the LORD God as he was walking in the garden in the cool of the day, and they hid" (Genesis 3:8). Perhaps that's why we still feel so close to God in a garden. Perhaps we were made that way. Perhaps our hearts still yearn for what we lost.

THOUGHTS TO PONDER
- ❀ Is there a place that always makes me feel close to God?
- ❀ Could I find a special place to meditate in daily, a place to walk and talk with God?

"Once while St. Francis of Assisi was hoeing his garden, he was asked, 'What would you do if you were suddenly to learn that you were to die at sunset today?' He replied, 'I would finish hoeing my garden.' "—Source Unknown

PRAYER GARDEN

Have you ever considered designing a corner of your garden for prayer and meditation, a special place for you and God to meet every day? Even if you don't have space for a "real" garden, perhaps you can create a patio or desk garden. Close your eyes and imagine the sights, sounds, and smells you would like in your prayer garden. Can you make it real?

A Prayer Garden might include
- A bench
- Fragrant plants
- A trellis for privacy
- A small pond or birdbath

A Patio Garden could consist of
- A deck chair
- Potted and hanging plants
- A bird cage

A Desk Garden might start with
- A plant tray
- A small sand garden
- A desk fountain

God built a garden in Eden for a place to talk with Adam and Eve. Gardens are good places to talk to God.

RSVPs

Christ tells several interesting stories about parties in the New Testament. Have you ever wondered what the people in Jesus' day must have been like? Did they go in for parties in a big way, or were they simply avid readers of the local society column? In one story, Jesus relates the tale of a local dignitary who decides to throw a big party at his country villa. His invitations are hand delivered, presumably engraved on the finest Egyptian parchment. The menu for the banquet is carefully selected. The hired chef has ordered delicacies from Persia to Ethiopia. The tapestries are hung, the lights are strung, the tables are set. One by one the RSVPs from the local gentry are returned. One guest is closing on a big real estate deal and sends his regrets. Another is heading for a honeymoon on the Mediterranean with his trophy bride and begs to be excused. Another is taking his brand-new team of oxen out for a test spin, etc., etc. The host is horrified. He has planned and prepared the social event of the season, and none of his invited guests can be bothered to show up. As I understand the parable, the invited guests represent good, church-going, religious people. In other words, us. I guess we're a pretty busy group. What a shame! (See Luke 14.)

THOUGHTS TO PONDER

❀ What is my payoff for staying busy all the time? Does it make me feel important, needed, secure?

❀ Is it possible that I have become so comfortable being a part of the right group, right church, right family, etc. that I might put off an opportunity to get to know Jesus better?

"Nothing makes you more tolerant of a neighbor's noisy party than being there."
—Franklin P. Jones

SAYING NO

Do you have a hard time saying No? Saying No seems to be a problem for most women. We feel almost compelled to say Yes to whatever we are asked to do. But it is not reasonable to expect to be able to do everything well when we are scheduled to the max. Something will suffer. Usually it is us. If you need help saying No, the following advice might be helpful:

1. **Never say Yes on the spot.** Always agree to think it over and get back with the answer later. If you have to say No, it at least appears as if you wanted to help, and you have bought some time to prepare a gracious regret.
2. **Is it something you can do well?** If you have been asked to do something that you know you do not have the talent or inclination to do well, politely decline.
3. **Do you have the time to do it justice?** Even if you want to help out but don't have the time to make a positive contribution, it is better to say No than to let everyone down.
4. **Is it something you would like to do?** If you have been asked to do something you are truly interested in and passionate about, take some time to put together the questions you have about the task or project before saying Yes.
5. **Will it help you reach other goals?** Volunteering is a great way to broaden your contacts, meet more people, stretch and add new skills. Make sure you understand your commitment and are willing to follow through.

Go to the Highways

After receiving several disappointing RSVPs to his party, the biblical host in Christ's parable is understandably upset. (See Luke 14.) Wine is cooling in the cellar, an ox is roasting on the spit, the musicians are waiting in the hall, the staff is standing by, but the invited guests have left him cooling his heels in an empty hall. The Lord of the Manor's face is clouded with disappointment. A banquet has been prepared. A banquet will be served! He orders his servants to town. Every poor beggar that has ever blemished the community with his dirty, unwashed, uncouth, presence is now invited to the finest banquet the Lord can serve. They are escorted to the elegantly laid tables; their feet are washed by the maidservants; their cups are filled with imported wine; the first course is served. "Excuse me, my Lord," the major-domo whispers, "there are still empty tables. The kitchen is overflowing with food."

"Go out to the roads and country lanes," the Lord orders, "and make them come in, so that my house will be full!" And the band played all night, and they danced and sang and laughed until the wee hours of the morning. And nobody left hungry or thirsty or sad or bored. In fact, nobody left at all. And they all lived happily ever after with the Lord. The End.

THOUGHTS TO PONDER

❀ With whom do I identify with in the parable, the respectable citizens or the disfigured beggars?

❀ Will heaven be full? With whom will heaven be full?

"If a free society cannot help the many who are poor, it cannot save the few who are rich."
—John F. Kennedy

NEIGHBORHOODS

No matter what neighborhood or community you live in, there are individuals who reside pretty much on the fringes. We get so used to our own "group," whether it is in our church or in our communities, that we are sometimes completely "blind" to members outside our little sphere. Take a little time to open your eyes to the "outsiders" this week. Are there ways you can include them in your circle? Often the best missionary work we can do is making friends.

At Church
❀ Invite a family you don't know well home for Sabbath dinner.
❀ Ask a new member to assist in a social event.
❀ Sit with someone new at potluck.

At Work
❀ Invite someone new to join your "lunch group."
❀ Include someone you wouldn't normally include on a group project.
❀ Suggest a new staff member to help out with the community fundraiser.

In the Neighborhood
❀ Drop off some homemade cookies to the new neighbors.
❀ Host a backyard get-together.
❀ Arrange a play date with the new family's kids and yours.

Party Poopers

In the medieval poem *Beowulf,* an ogre lurking in the caves below the town is enraged by the sound of laughter coming from a celebration taking place in the mead hall above. The beast in his misery cannot tolerate the sounds of joy. He crawls out of his lair and descends upon the town in a murderous rage, slaughtering the revelers. Now there's a party pooper for you!

You and I might be a little more subtle. We might express a few concerns to our coworker about the crushing pressures of his new promotion. We might sadly remind our best friend of a string of failed relationships when she falls head over heels in love with someone new. We might call it concern or tough love. We might say, "If your friends won't tell you, who will?" We might even say, "The truth hurts." We would be so full of phony baloney! What hurts is watching someone else get the promotion we deserved. What hurts is watching someone as totally undeserving as our best friend in the throes of a wild romance when our own relationships are stale and going nowhere. What hurts is the sound of party revelers when we are lurking about in the dark caves of self-pity, resentment, and regret. Unhappiness is intolerant of joy. It will kill joy whenever possible.

THOUGHTS TO PONDER

❀ Have I ever been ambushed by a friend when telling her my good news?

❀ Are friends who regularly "rain on my parade" really friends worth having at all?

"He who fights with monsters might take care lest he thereby become a monster. And if you gaze for long into an abyss, the abyss gazes also into you."—Friedrich Nietzsche

SPIRITUAL MONSTERS AND MENTORS

Julia Cameron, in her book *The Artist's Way*, encourages blocked artists to identify their creative monsters and acknowledge the damage they have done. By "creative monsters" she refers to those individuals close to us who have discouraged us from realizing the full potential of our talents. Often these friends, family members, and/or teachers are well-meaning but misguided. They prevent us from fully developing by dismissing or criticizing our gifts and talents at vulnerable moments. Sometimes it is years before we build up the courage to try again.

The same is true of spiritual seekers. We often approach truth with a lot of "spiritual monsters" buried deep in our psyches waiting to crawl out of their caves and criticize our spiritual lives. No wonder there are many "blocked" Christians, as well as "blocked" artists. What spiritual monsters have you had to contend with in your life? To borrow an exercise from Cameron's book, take out a sheet of paper and draw a line down the middle of the paper. On the right-hand side, write down the names of those individuals who have always been there for you, who have encouraged you, who have nourished you in God's goodness. These are your spiritual mentors. Thank God for blessing your life with them. On the left-hand side of the page, write the names of those individuals who have not nourished you but have criticized, rebuked, and ridiculed your attempts to serve God. These are your spiritual monsters, even if they are disguised as friends or family members. It is not our responsibility to judge these individuals, but it is helpful to understand that they cannot aid us in our spiritual growth. We can make the choice not to grant them influence in our lives. We have a mighty Champion ready to do battle with even our most persistent and deep-seated fears. Jesus Christ is ready and willing to heal us. He will bind our painful memories and sorrows and make us whole if we let Him. We were created to enjoy a relationship with Him. He can make it so!

Party Invitations

Once upon a time in the sixties, literary darling Truman Capote threw a lavish, black-and-white masquerade party at the New York City Plaza Hotel. Legend has it that he agonized over the guest list, adding and deleting names up until the moment the postman arrived. Luminaries from the financial, arts, entertainment, and the most elite social circles were blessed with the coveted invitations. Those who didn't make the cut planned overseas vacations to explain their conspicuous absence. The star-studded party was, by all accounts, a fabulous, never-to-be-repeated success, not even by Capote himself. Capote's attempt, some years later, to throw a second black-and-white masquerade was an embarrassing affair, more notable for those who declined to attend than those who did. By then, Capote and his writing had fallen out of fashion with the New York Glitterati, and he was seen as what he had always been, a poor boy from Alabama, an outsider, an interloper, a passing fad. He was just a literary genius, of course, not a permanent member of New York's social elite.

No matter how successful, how important, how sought after we are, don't we all experience terrible insecurity from time to time? If people really knew us, would they still want us around? What if we were unmasked, and people were to find out how afraid and lonely and insecure we really were? Surprisingly enough, the One who knows our every flaw, wart, and hidden disfigurement most intimately is the One most desirous of our company.

If I go and prepare a place for you, I will come back and take you to be with me that you also may be where I am (John 14:3).

THOUGHTS TO PONDER
- ❀ Have I experienced complete and total acceptance?
- ❀ Do I know how to give complete and total acceptance?

"The closing years of life are like the end of a masquerade party, when the masks are dropped."—Arthur Schopenhauer, German philosopher, 1788-1860

THEME PARTY

Children can hardly wait for summer to start, but as moms well know, halfway into the summer, the kids become bored, restless, and lonesome for their school friends. Agree to let them plan a summer get-together. A theme party in the backyard is fun but not expensive. If you let the kids make the party plans (within reason), they will stay happily occupied for several days. Limit the party to three hours. Consider one of the following easy backyard party themes:

- **Beach Party.** Everything wet! Kiddie pools, slip and slides, and water guns. Decorate with umbrellas, beach balls, and volleyballs. Everybody brings a towel and a change of clothes for after the fun is over. Serve easy beach food—hot dogs and cold drinks.
- **Matchbox Car Rally.** Set up the tracks outside. The more tracks the better. Get hubby to set up a few additional inclines or trick tracks. Invite every kid to bring favorite matchbox racers. Set up free-for-all practice until the races start. Organize meets on all the tracks. Pizza and drinks are easy food fare.
- **Summer Theatre.** Let your young ones pick a play or even write one. Send out the parts in advance. Fabric remnants, old clothes, and hats make great costumes. Let the drama troupe run through their parts while you set up lawn chairs for the parents. String a clothesline for the curtain. Popcorn, sandwiches, and chips are all the food you need. Plan the party near sundown and spotlight with flashlights for added drama.

Sabbath Was Made for (Wo)Man

Can you imagine what it would be like to start every Friday sundown with a clean house, potluck casserole already prepared and in the fridge, and the kids' church clothes neatly pressed and laid out for the morning? Sabbath morning would start with a leisurely family breakfast. No lost ribbons or misplaced socks. Everyone would be calm and relaxed on the drive to church. A thought-provoking Sabbath School discussion and an inspiring sermon would be followed by a warm fellowship dinner. You would arrive home in time to change into your walking shoes for a brisk nature hike. As your trudge back to the house, the sun is just beginning to set, and you gather your family around for a few songs and a prayer thanking God for setting aside such a refreshing and relaxing day for us.

Are you laughing hysterically or weeping at this point? Maybe a little bit of both. When did it get so out of control? Why has Sabbath become one of the most stressful days of the week for so many of us? Do we say Yes to too many church responsibilities? Are we too busy to really prepare for the Sabbath? Could we use a little help here? I think the answer again is Yes. Sabbath is supposed to be a special day to connect with God, our church, and our family. If that's not happening for us, perhaps we need to make some changes, get some help, assign some chores, and turn down a few extra duties. After all, Sabbath was made for (wo)man, not (wo)man for the Sabbath.

THOUGHTS TO PONDER
- How would I like to begin and celebrate Sabbath each week?
- What changes can I start to put in place to improve my Sabbath experience?

BROCCOLI CASSEROLE
FRESH PRODUCE

Use market or garden-fresh broccoli for this casserole, if available. Preparation time: 20 minutes. Baking time: 60 minutes. Serves 8-10.

Pantry Items
Canned shallots (2 cans)
Condensed mushroom soup (1 can)
Chicken-style seasoning (1 Tbsp.)
Light mayonnaise (1 cup)

Fresh Items
Three stalks of fresh broccoli
  (or 2 boxes frozen broccoli)
Sweet onion (1 large, chopped)
Fresh basil (2 Tbsp., chopped)
Fresh garlic (3 cloves, chopped)
Shredded cheddar cheese (1 8-oz. bag)
Light sour cream (1 cup)

DIRECTIONS
If using fresh broccoli, cut into bite-size pieces. In a large bowl, combine broccoli, chopped onion, basil, garlic, and drained shallots. Set aside. In a medium bowl, combine sour cream, mayonnaise, mushroom soup, and seasoning. Mix well. Pour mixture into broccoli and vegetables and stir gently. Fold in shredded cheese. Pour into casserole and cover with foil. May store overnight in fridge, but bring to room temperature before baking. Bake at 350° F for 60 minutes. Remove foil after 30 minutes. Casserole is done when center bubbles and broccoli is tender.

Let Me Hear Joy

We are "fearfully and wonderfully made" (Psalm 139:14), as the psalmist puts it. We have a God-given capacity for joy, which expresses itself in a wide range of emotions: delight, laughter, exuberance, contentment, affection, passion. And in the center is God, our Creator and Lord and the One for whom we were created. He is the One who loves us and delights in us, the One who was willing to redeem us, whatever the cost. I cannot believe this God desired to empty heaven so that we would live small, constrained lives focused on burdens and sorrows. I have seen Christians so focused on not loving this world that they lose the ability to love the Creator of this magnificent world.

How sad God's heart must be to see perpetually sober-faced Christians who are afraid to claim the abundance of gifts He is thrusting toward them. It would be like throwing a birthday party for a little girl and watching her hold her emotions tightly in check as she solemnly opened one package after another, determined not to "enjoy" them too much. Wouldn't we much prefer that the child rip her presents open with joy and squeal with delight? Why wouldn't God?

THOUGHTS TO PONDER

❀ Do I allow myself to enjoy the good things God has blessed me with?

❀ How do I model joy, praise, and divine gratefulness for my children?

"We find the most terrible form of atheism, not in the militant and passionate struggle against the idea of God himself, but in the practical atheism of everyday living, in indifference and torpor. We often encounter these forms of atheism among those who are formally Christians."
—Nicolai A. Berdyaev

HEAVENLY TRAVELOGUE
INSIDE OR OUTSIDE ACTIVITY

Grades: 5th to Adult
Materials Needed:
  Lots of imagination

The participants enact a travelogue based on an imaginary trip to heaven. Each participant chooses a portion of the heavenly travelogue. The reports are presented as if the participant has just returned from heaven and is presenting a travelogue to a group of people interested in visiting there. Each reporter focuses on a different aspect of heaven. This game can be played impromptu, or the assignments can be handed out ahead of time. No presentation should last longer than two minutes. Assign a narrator to monitor and introduce the reporters.

Heavenly Travelogue Cast:
Narrator   Introduces each reporter and monitors time
Reporter 1 The Trip to Heaven—transportation and scenic stops
Reporter 2 Dining—food and eating establishments in heaven
Reporter 3 Entertainment—heavenly shows
Reporter 4 Local Color—people and customs in heaven
Reporter 5 Flora and Fauna—types of animals and plants in heaven
Reporter 6 Historical Interest—places and points of heavenly interest

Feasts

In the 1950 short story "Babette's Feast," by Danish writer Isak Dinesen, a destitute housekeeper wins the lottery and decides to spend her entire fortune on the preparation of one lavish meal. The invited guests are the members of her employer's small but devout church group. As boats begin delivering extraordinary shipments of gastronomical delicacies to the small village on the rugged Danish coast, the church members become suspicious and wary. They hold an emergency meeting. They decide that in the end they must partake of Babette's feast, but they vow not to enjoy it. They will simply chew and swallow it. Babette is aware that her generosity is viewed as frivolous and ungodly, and that it will most likely be lost on the elderly members of the small religious sect; however, she is not deterred.

What her employers do not know is that Babette was once a celebrated Parisian chef before falling on hard times. The lottery has provided her with one last opportunity to set aside the preparation of gruel and fish soup, the standard fare of the two elderly sisters she works for, and prepare a rare feast. On the appointed day the guests arrive, grim and determined. Years of pious bickering and petty quarrels have taken their toll on the small church. Members, holding grudges and resentments against one another for untold years, gather around the table like sullen children. Babette begins to serve. As the church members partake of one mouthwatering delicacy after another, their resolve begins to melt. Faces lose their taunt expressions. Gradually smiles begin to appear and are shyly returned. With each successive course, the mood lightens. By the end of the evening, the small group raises their voices together in a hymn of praise, arm in arm, forgiving and forgiven. The love and unity that has evaded them through years of study and prayer, blossoms suddenly in the outpouring of Babette's sumptuous, unselfish gift.

She has poured perfume on my feet. Therefore, I tell you, her many sins have been forgiven—for she loved much (Luke 7:46, 47).

THOUGHTS TO PONDER
- ❀ Why do religious groups often seem to be more prone to bickering than harmony?
- ❀ How can we put aside our differences and learn to cherish one another?

"He who distinguishes the true savor of his food can never be a glutton; he who does not cannot be otherwise."—Henry David Thoreau

DINING ALFRESCO

Whether it's a picnic, a backyard barbeque, or a candlelight dinner in the garden, eating a meal in the open air with friends and family seems to encourage special intimacy and closeness. Following are a few alfresco dining tips to keep the occasion stress free:

❀ **Wind Control.** Wind is almost always going to be a factor, so plan for it. Use pretty rocks, seashells, or other weighted objects to keep tablecloths and napkins from blowing away.

❀ **Sun Control.** During the day the direct sun can be brutal on both food and diners. Think about shade trees, beach umbrellas, and stringing sheets as pretty makeshift awnings.

❀ **Pest Control.** There is almost no way to avoid the little peskies. A few ideas to minimize the annoyance: Screen tops and table tents will keep flies out of the potato salad. Citronella lamps minimize mosquitoes at night plus provide a very romantic atmosphere. Setting table legs in tin cans filled with kerosene eliminates the crawlies from the buffet.

❀ **Easy Cleanup.** Set up a large lidded container with heavy-duty trash liners for easy trash control. Set a bucket of soapy water beside the trash can to drop washable utensils in.

Festivals

Ancient Hebrew law designated several national religious festivals: festivals of deliverance, thanksgiving, repentance, and even restoration of lost inheritances. At these festivals the Jewish nation gathered together, often for several days, to celebrate God's care and presence in their daily lives. During the celebrations, the Jews not only observed the ceremonial rituals performed in the temple but also participated in each event as a family unit as well, with specific ceremonies and rituals to enact together. There was no opportunity to remain just a festival observer. Everyone was a festival participant.

Modern Christianity, particularly Protestantism, has eschewed a lot of ceremony and ritual. Our religious observances tend to be spare and refined in comparison to ancient Israel. We appreciate a certain economy to our worship. Christianity observes few festivals involving active personal participation. Christmas and Easter qualify, but even these celebrations have been refined into beautiful observances presented by a few for the rest of us to observe. Communion and the ordinances of humility are two of the few participatory rituals we celebrate. But perhaps *celebrate* is too strong a word. A festival implies more than passive observance. It implies active participation, exuberance, celebration!

THOUGHTS TO PONDER

❀ Christians have so much to celebrate. Why does celebration seem so foreign to us?

❀ What personal ways could I find to celebrate Sabbath or communion with my family and friends?

"You will sing as on the night you celebrate a holy festival; your hearts will rejoice as when people go up with flutes to the mountain of the LORD, to the Rock of Israel."—Isaiah 30:29

SACRED CELEBRATIONS

Celebrations are an important ritual in life. They bind our memories to ideals, family, and community. Developing sacred memories is an important part of growing up. Those memories keep us connected to our faith and our heritage even during dark periods in our life. Perhaps that's why God instituted so many celebrations for ancient Israel. Consider ways you can celebrate God's goodness with your family. Pick celebrations that can become family traditions that you will enjoy repeating year after year.

❊ Celebrate an adult family member's birthday with a candlelight Communion supper. Invite friends and a pastor to officiate.

❊ Pick a "Widows Mite" day. Scour the house for loose change and donate proceeds to a charity.

❊ Begin the Sabbath by allowing each member to light a candle and share God's blessings.

❊ Host a Saturday-evening muffin bake to commemorate the miracle of the loaves and fishes. Distribute baked goods to the homeless Sunday morning.

❊ Plan an annual family camping trip in conjunction with ancient Israel's Festival of Tents to celebrate God's deliverance from Egypt and soon deliverance from this world.

I Am Well Pleased

Nobody got it. It was probably His most difficult cross to bear—and He would bear many. He enjoyed fame, notoriety, admiration, affection, even love, but not even those few who loved Him got it. If it ever came up, they politely overlooked it as if it were a bizarre hiccup in His persona, one they hoped He'd outgrow. After all, He was young, and He was gifted. There was no doubt about that. He could change water into wine, heal the sick, and walk on water. That He claimed to have been sent to die seemed a little theatrical perhaps but understandable, an easily overlooked peculiarity. Certainly He had plenty of enemies. His friends tried to assure Him that they would stand by Him, that they would protect Him, that they would keep Him safe. They never got it. No matter how many ways He tried to explain it to them, they insisted on misunderstanding Him. Their big leap of faith was admitting He was the Son of God. They couldn't quite get their minds around the idea that He was also the Lamb of God. They were firmly fixed on the crown, not on the cross. He would not fulfill their dreams; He had a different agenda. They would be shocked, surprised, taken off guard. They would scatter like leaves in the wind, and He couldn't help them. In this respect He failed them. It must have broken His heart. Then the Father spoke, "This is my Son, whom I love; with him I am well pleased. Listen to him!" (Matthew 17:5).

THOUGHTS TO PONDER

❀ Have I ever failed to reach and protect the ones I love the most?
❀ Can I conceive of a God who loves me and accepts me and never blames me?

"Love is an act of endless forgiveness, a tender look which becomes a habit."
—Peter Ustinov

UNFORGIVEN

In Clint Eastwood's Oscar-winning 1992 movie *Unforgiven,* an old gunman attempts to retire to rear his children in a remote corner of the Wyoming frontier, where he hopes no one will find him. Of course, he doesn't succeed, and his bad deeds return to haunt him. In the movie, all parties are flawed and less than heroic. They are all unforgiven. As Christians, how do we face our failures? How do we ask for forgiveness? How do we grant forgiveness?

1. Only God grants forgiveness. Unless someone who has wronged me requests my forgiveness, I am powerless to grant forgiveness. But I can surrender my hate.
2. When I sin against another, I need to take full ownership of my actions, request that person's forgiveness, and make things right as much as possible.
3. I need to understand that not all failure is sin. Sometimes failure happens in spite of my best efforts. Even Christ was not able to save everyone He came in contact with. Some things are out of my control.
4. I need to put things in perspective. I cannot beat myself up continually, or another person for that matter. It takes too much energy. This is a sinful world. We will hurt and be hurt by one another. We can only turn humbly to God for help and comfort.
5. If I still cannot put a failure behind me and move on, I need to discover what keeps me stuck. What's in it for me to keep dwelling on a failure, mine or others'? Have I allowed this failure to define my life, to give me an identity, to garner sympathy?
6. When someone requests my forgiveness, I owe that person my complete and total forgiveness, but I do not owe him or her a negation of the consequences. Even God does not always choose to intervene in the consequences of our bad actions.
7. When I ask for forgiveness, I should not expect for a negation of my actions either—just an acknowledgement that I understand and regret my actions.

Banquet Tables

Do you remember academy banquets? Have you ever stayed up all night with a group of friends, trying to transform a cafeteria or gymnasium into something romantic or elegant? At that tender age, we all longed for a taste of sophisticated glamour. We were anxious to exercise our adult personas. After hours painting backdrops and stringing lights, streamers, and balloons, you may have dragged yourself home in the wee hours of the morning, exhausted, under the firm conviction that it didn't matter how much decorating one did; it was still the cafeteria.

That evening as you arrived for the festivities, hair lacquered firmly in place above your head, high heels allowing you to tower over your nervous date, you may have ducked through the glittering archway into another world. In the illusion conjured by the dim light of the candles reflecting only the shimmering decorations, tables covered in white paper, set with champagne glasses and elaborately folded napkins, it may have seemed as if you had been transported suddenly into a more grown-up world. The hard-won ambiance appeared to change awkward teenagers into newly made adults. Of course, the food was still from the cafeteria, the emcee's jokes probably weren't funny, and the entertainment may have been uneven; but for one evening you shed the awkwardness of adolescence and stepped into the woman you were becoming. It was bittersweet magic filled with great expectations and towering insecurities.

Someday soon, we will experience that transformation again. As we shed our awkward, imperfect, unsightly mortal shell for immortality, arrayed in His righteousness, we will sit at the banquet table He has prepared for us, with His love a rainbow canopy above us, and His universe a carpet of stars at our feet. And we will finally experience the woman we were created to be.

THOUGHTS TO PONDER
- ❀ Have I ever contemplated what kind of woman I was created to be?
- ❀ Can I claim part of that power and beauty now, knowing He will complete it when He comes?

"It is an illusion that youth is happy, an illusion of those who have lost it."
—W. Somerset Maugham, British novelist, 1874-1965

WOMAN POWER

Women of God wield great power, but it is not power as the world understands power. It is not an obvious power such as wealth, position, or beauty. It is an inner power, born of the Spirit, a power that serves, that endures. Unless a woman is willing to submit her power to God's will, it remains a small, ineffectual desire. But when it is fused with the will of God, it is an awesome force for good. It's like falling backward into the arms of someone you trust. It is a belief that:

1. God will never take me anyplace I would not choose to go if I could see the end from the beginning.
2. God will make clear His will. I do not need to anticipate Him.
3. God will give me the talents I need to complete the tasks He desires me to do.
4. God will give me the life experiences I need to benefit others.
5. God will turn every wall into a stepping stone.
6. God understands my weaknesses and will sustain me.
7. In God's economy there are no wasted experiences. Every wrong turn, failure, inadequacy is an opportunity for His grace and glory to abound.
8. Obedience to His will is the path to joy, not to drudgery.
9. Through sacrifice I exchange my rocks for His diamonds. There is no sacrifice—only the illusion of sacrifice.
10. By His grace I can do anything.

Taste and See That I Am Good

When we were younger than we are now, we probably thought that being good meant missing out on real life. The cool kids had cars, boyfriends, parties, and great clothes. They didn't worry about rules. They laughed at authority. They made their own rules. They were the only ones having a good time—or so we thought. Most of us struggled with pimples, perpetual body envy, social awkwardness, and massive insecurities. Of course, it was all just an illusion. It didn't really matter what group you belonged to in high school, there was always a group that was older, hipper, cooler.

It doesn't take very many years to realize that partying is no way to build an inhabitable life. Those friends of ours still stuck on the party circuit have burned through their youth at lightning speed. Too much casual sex, casual drugs, casual jobs, and ugly words such as *alcoholism, divorce, addictions,* and *abortions,* take the cool right out of hip. Burned out and burned up, realizing too late that commitment, loyalty, and dependability are the stuff real life is made of. If we could only understand that God wants desperately to give us every good gift, every happiness, every good thing in life. "Taste and see that I am good," He entreats us. Let Me give you the love of a family, the loyalty of friends, the affection of children. Let Me give you joy and laughter. Let Me give you peace and love. Let Me be your God, and all these things will be added unto you.

THOUGHTS TO PONDER

❀ How can I help my teenagers understand that God wants them to enjoy every good thing in life?

❀ Can we help our teenagers understand that life without God is a life full of pain?

"The American ideal is youth—handsome, empty youth.
—Henry Miller, American author, 1891-1980

DAUGHTERS OF GOD

Mother-daughter relationships are among the most enduring relationships on this earth. They are also one of the most complicated. We experience many of the same life experiences but on such disparate timelines that we are certain we do not understand each other! Building bridges of communication and trust can span the timeline of our lives. A few tips for the journey:

❀ If you can talk to your daughter about God, you can talk to her about anything. Talk to your daughter about God early and often—and listen well.
❀ Don't try to relive your youth through your daughter. This advice is almost a cliché, but I think it is still important because the temptation is so great.
❀ Don't wrap your ego into your daughter's choices. You are separate entities, and you are each entitled to make it on your own merits.
❀ Find things you can enjoy together. Time together binds relationships. Love without sharing is never quite satisfactory. Never let life get so busy that you sacrifice that precious time together.

As a Grandfather Gives Good Gifts

I know it's not theologically correct. The correct phrase would be "as a father gives good gifts." But I think the heart and soul of the verse is not diminished by the exchange. Grandfathers adore granddaughters. They probably have for as long as there have been granddaughters for grandfathers to spoil. Adam no doubt spoiled every single one of his granddaughters. My grandfathers spoiled me thoroughly with no apologies. Saturday-night trips out for old-fashioned root-beer floats in the frosted mug, circus tickets with front-row seats, Sunday afternoons at Yankee Stadium, trips to the country to collect cattails, long rides on the tractor—just the two of us.

They probably spent more money on me than they should have, but what I remember most is the time they spent with me. Grandfather gifts involve time. They are not the type of gifts you unwrap and then go off to play with by yourself. Grandfather gifts are enjoyed together. By now I have lost most of my childhood gifts. But I will never lose the wonderful memories of the time I spent with my grandfathers. Those were times that made me feel special, beautiful, safe, and important. So, if you will permit me to paraphrase the verse, "If your grandfathers, being mere mortal men, know how to give wonderful, loving gifts, how much more does your heavenly father desire to pour out the riches of heaven for you?" (See Matthew 7 and Luke 11.)

THOUGHTS TO PONDER
- When was the last time I gave my children the gift of my undivided attention?
- Am I able to believe that God loves and adores me in the most tender way? If I could believe that, how would that change my life?

SEVEN-LAYER SALAD
SEASONAL PRODUCE

This is one of the few garden salad recipes that making ahead of time actually improves the flavor. Preparation time: 20 minutes. Refrigerate: 4 hours or overnight. Serves 10-12.

Pantry Items
Garbanzos or chick peas (1 can, well drained)
Thousand Island salad dressing (1 16-oz. bottle)
Imitation bacon bits (1 cup)
Salt and pepper (to taste)

Fresh Items
Lettuce or mixed salad greens (8 cups)
Scallions (1 cup, chopped)
Peas, fresh or frozen (1 cup)
Shredded cheddar cheese (1 cup)

DIRECTIONS
If using fresh peas, blanch peas in a bath of boiling salted water for 2 minutes, drain, and rinse with cold water. Set peas aside. Tear or shred salad greens into bite-size pieces. Spread two cups of salad greens on the bottom of a 9" x 12" glass casserole dish. Sprinkle lightly with salt and pepper. Spread the garbanzos or chick peas evenly over the salad greens. Add a second layer of 2 cups salad greens; lightly sprinkle salt and pepper. Spread the chopped scallions evenly over the salad greens. Repeat process for third layer with salad greens and peas. Top with remaining 2 cups of salad greens. Drizzle bottle of Thousand Island salad dressing over salad. Sprinkle with shredded cheese. Cover and refrigerate for four hours or overnight. Before serving, sprinkle imitation bacon bits evenly over salad.

SUBSTITUTIONS: There are a number of substitutions you can make to the Seven-Layer Salad, depending on your family's preferences or what you have on hand. You can substitute 1 can diced beets for garbanzos; 1 cup of blanched edamame (shelled soybeans) for peas; 2 cups lite mayonnaise for Thousand Island salad dressing; I cup of feta cheese crumbles for shredded cheddar cheese (omit bacon bits), 1 tablespoon fresh chopped basil per layer in place of black pepper.

NOTE: To keep salad crisp, make sure all vegetables are *well drained* before assembling the salad.

Showers of Blessings

I once lived in Africa, in the rainforest that rings the southern-most side of the Sahara Desert. Although most of the year was a hot, wet, and humid existence when nothing ever quite dried out and mold was a pestilence, during three months out of every year the rains stopped. The rains stopped completely, not a mist, not a sprinkle, not a drop of dew. The winds from the north blew in a fine red dust that coated everything, even our eyelashes and noses. The lush colors of the rainforest wilted. The trees and villages, covered in a thick layer of dust, looked as if they had been forgotten and neglected by the celestial housekeepers. The water supplies dwindled dangerously. Baths became shared luxuries. The sun beat down mercilessly from the cloudless skies. Finally, when we felt we could bear it no longer, the winds changed. You could smell it in the air. The storms from the south were approaching. The sky turned black; the wind blew like a siren heralding the rains. Our parched spirits took on new life. We rushed outside. We lifted our arms to the sky. We threw our bodies against the wind. The rains were coming! What joy, what rejoicing! And as the rains finally reached us, we leaped and twirled in the blessed wetness. Showers of blessings—I know what that means. Showers of blessings are what our Father desires to bestow upon our parched and wilted sprits. Lift your arms to the heavens!

THOUGHTS TO PONDER

❀ If my life feels parched and dry, where do I find the showers of God's blessings?

❀ Are there memories of past dry spells that ended with God's goodness that can sustain me now?

MEMENTO BOX
OUTSIDE ACTIVITY

Ages: 5 to Adult
Materials Needed:
    Sturdy canvas or net bag for collecting
    Butterfly net and/or bug box
    Medium-size craft box
    Quilt batting (large enough to cover bottom of the craft box)
    Straight pins
    Manila envelope

1. **The Nature Walk.** The most important aspect of this activity is to locate a place for a nature walk where you will be allowed to collect specimens such as rocks, pinecones, beetles, butterflies, moss, and wildflowers, or, if you are at a beach, shells, coral, rocks, and driftwood.
2. **The Box.** The second task is to locate a sturdy box of the right size to display the collection. Craft stores sell a variety of cardboard craft boxes. Look for a wide box, not too high. Purchase enough quilt batting to cover the bottom of the box with a layer of batting. (You will probably have plenty left over for another craft project.)
3. **Preparing the Specimens.** Preparation of specimens is a critical task. Shells should be soaked in a bleach solution and dried in the sun to avoid unpleasant odors. Plants, such as wild flowers and leaves, need to be pressed flat between the pages of an old phone book. Paint shells and pebbles with one or two coats of clear nail polish to simulate their colors when wet with surf.
4. **Assembling the Display.** Trace the shape of the box bottom with a marker onto the batting and cut to size. Line the bottom of the box with the batting. Arrange the specimens on the batting. Use straight pins to secure fragile items such as butterflies, beetles, and plants. Type or hand write labels on strips of paper and attach near specimen with a straight pin. Glue the envelope to the inside of the lid and place any brochures or maps of the area in the envelope. Label the top of the box with the place and date.

Wedding Party

Brides are fussed over and celebrated in every culture. It is no small affair to turn out a bride on her wedding day. Whether the wedding is taking place in Nairobi or Oslo or Kankakee, the hair, the costume, and the makeup are elaborately devised and executed by a staff of excited attendants. The wedding feast preparations begin months in advance. Everything from decorations to musicians is selected and planned out in careful detail. Something will undoubtedly go wrong.

Christ's first miracle was at a wedding. He turned their water into wine and their embarrassment into rejoicing. Apparently even the Creator of the universe couldn't bear to see a bride disappointed on her wedding day. There is something terribly touching and a little sentimental about that thought. I like this God of ours! And the fact that He refers to us as His bride is almost too incredible for words. What blind love is this that He would fuss over and celebrate the consummation of His love for us as if He were an adoring groom, as if we were the supreme object of His affection? A wedding feast awaits us that has been planned and prepared since the beginning of time. We will be attired in His righteousness, we will glow with His radiance, we will be beautiful because He has made us so!

THOUGHT TO PONDER

✿ Can I accept the gift of Christ's love and adoration, or am I still too wrapped up in my flaws and imperfections?

"When a wife has a good husband it is easily seen in her face."
—Johann Wolfgang Von Goethe, German poet, 1749-1832

ROSE GARDENS

There is no doubt that the rose is the queen of flowers, a title coined by Sappho in 600 B.C. Roses are irresistibly romantic. Writers have been rhapsodizing about roses since the time of the Babylonians. Three known rose varieties have a history that extends back to the time of Christ, making them among the most ancient plants still cultivated. Because of the rose's status, many gardeners believe that roses are difficult to cultivate. That is not necessarily so. An afternoon in the library or on the Internet will provide you with enough practical information to successfully cultivate a rose garden in your climate. Following are some ideas to get you started:

Hardy Rose Varieties. Referred to as "old garden roses," this variety can withstand freezing temperatures to minus 20° F. Some modern varieties bred for hardiness include Rugosa, Canadian Explorer, Meidiland, and Griffith Buck.

Ancient Rose Varieties. Several varieties, such as Gallica, Allba, and Damask roses, date back to the time of Christ.

Especially Fragrant Roses. Fragrant roses are found in all rose varieties. Following are some well-known fragrant favorites: Mister Lincoln, Auguste Renoir, Double Delight, Scentimental, Fragrant Cloud.

Types of Roses. Although hybrid roses are traditional rose bushes, roses come in many sizes from tiny, petite blossoms no larger than your thumb to large double blossoms resembling peonies. Some roses are climbers, perfect for arches and trellises, and some grow to the size of shrubs. You may find that experimenting with a container rose garden first is an easy and convenient way to become familiar with a variety of rose types.

Rose Sentiments. If you are a romantic, you might enjoy learning what message a rose color expresses: red—love; deep pink—gratitude; light pink—admiration; white—reverence; yellow—joy; orange—desire.

His Banner Over Me Is Love

Though I walk through the shadow of doubts, His banner over me is love. Though I travel strange roads and wander through detours, His banner over me is love. When I sink into self-doubt and inertia, still His banner over me is love. When I am overburdened and overscheduled, His banner over me is love. Whether I ignore Him or praise Him, His banner still surrounds me. I cannot lose Him. I cannot deny Him; He will sustain me still. I can only bow at His feet and pour my life out for Him. He will gather my failures and turn them into compassion. He will gather my doubts and press my hand deep into His wounded side. He will take my blackest sins and turn them into great love. He is my alchemist. He turns my base metals into gold, my sadness into rejoicing, my pain into gladness. I am His beloved child, and His banner over me is love.

I will boast all the more gladly about my weaknesses, so that Christ's power may rest on me. . . . For when I am weak, then I am strong (2 Corinthians 12:9, 10).

THOUGHTS TO PONDER

❀ What failures have I experienced that God has turned into blessings?

❀ Are there any failures that He has not yet transformed into something beautiful? When will I let go of my shame and allow Him to use even my worst failures for His glory?

"Every adversity, every failure, every heartache carries with it the seed of an equal or greater benefit."—Napoleon Hill, American writer, 1883-1970

FEAR OF FAILURE

No young person graduates from college eagerly anticipating failure. But failure is one of life's greatest blessings. We learn more from our failures than we do from our successes. We grow through our failures in ways that we could never grow through our victories. Should we aim for failure? Never! But neither should we fear failure. Fear of failure is infinitely more crippling to our lives and our careers than failure itself. Is fear of failure keeping you from achieving your potential? Is playing it safe keeping you stuck in a dead-end situation? Ask yourself the following questions:

* Do I enjoy my job, or am I just marking time?
* Am I learning valuable new skills, or am I stagnating?
* Am I being challenged, or am I underachieving?
* If I had the courage, what would I be doing with my life right now?
* Is a lack of skills, education, contacts, or funding holding me back?
* What positive steps can I take to get the skills, education, contacts, or funding I need?
* Am I passing up opportunities because I am afraid?

As the old song says, "Take it to the Lord in prayer." Talk to your family, examine your options, and then devise a game plan to move out of your rut. Even a good player may miss a few goals, but she makes a lot more than her teammate sitting on the bench! Life as a spectator sport is not very satisfying.

A Woman of Means

The phrase has an elegant turn to it. It implies independence, privilege, and household help. How many of us have that? Still, the notion of expecting to be provided and cared for in an unbroken succession from father to husband to son is probably over— and for the best. A cage is still a cage, gilded or not. To be totally dependent on anyone but God is not a healthful adult choice. According to the description of the wife of noble character in Proverbs 31, every woman should cultivate business savvy along with domestic skills. Not only is the celebrated woman admired for her cooking, sewing, and childrearing skills, but she is equally admired for effective staff management, merchandizing savvy, real estate deals, and financial investments. As we read the chapter in Proverbs, it becomes clear that the Bible modeled the successful female executive some three to four thousand years ago. Talk about being ahead of its time! Perhaps God has always seen women as complete, not one-sided, creatures, created to exercise both the heart and the mind, competent in the marketplace as well as the home.

Her children arise and call her blessed; her husband also, and he praises her (Proverbs 31:28).

Give her the reward she has earned, and let her works bring her praise at the city gate (Proverbs 31:31).

THOUGHTS TO PONDER
- Have I accepted my pursuit of excellence in my chosen profession as a God-given, not a selfish, desire?
- Have I ever sabotaged myself professionally out of misplaced fear of success?

"You can have it all. You can have a family and a career. The variable is time."—Dr. June Scobee Rodgers, commencement address, Southern Adventist University, May 12, 2002

TIME MANAGEMENT

A lot of terrific books are available, such as the *The One Minute Manager* by Kenneth Blanchard, to help professionals make effective use of their time. An entire industry is built around personal organizers and electronic PDAs, a testimony to our era's underlying conviction that "time is money." What we may have overlooked is that "time is life." If we don't learn to balance our time, we have no life, and all the personal organizers in the world can't help us. I've learned that there are only five areas that need my attention every day. I call them my "Critical Five." I have learned that it is a bad idea to allow anything to squeeze these critical five areas of my life, even other "fives."

1. **Daily Meditation.** Daily time alone with God gives my life focus.
2. **Personal Time.** Every day I need some personal time. It recharges my battery.
3. **Romance.** My marriage requires daily, loving attention. It gives my life joy.
4. **Children.** My kids require my undivided attention at least once a day. It gives me peace.
5. **Career.** My professional life requires an honest day's work. It gives me satisfaction.

At the Feet of the Master

Mary of Magdala is one of the most intriguing and perplexing female characters in the Bible. What little we know of her history is not admirable. Although Mary's family home was in Bethany, she is forever known as Mary Magdalene because of an infamous stay in Magdala as a prostitute. How she ended up there is not clear. Some biblical scholars believe there is evidence of incest between her and her powerful Uncle Simon. Perhaps she was a teenage runaway. In any case, Magdala is where Christ happened upon her. By then Mary was in bad shape. The Bible says that Jesus cast the demons out of her seven times. (See Luke 8:2.) Was she suffering from dementia, addictions, self-loathing? It's impossible to know what her demons were, but that they had eroded and nearly destroyed her soul is certain.

Christ forgave her and rescued her, but it didn't take. Mary was not an easy or sympathetic convert. She chose to continue to return to her demons time and time again. And time and time again Christ sought her out and rescued her from her self-destructive choices. It's puzzling why Christ doted on her the way He did. Apparently her sister and the disciples were also mystified and a little jealous. When Martha complained about Mary's refusal to help out in the kitchen, she didn't get the support she was expecting. When Simon and Judas criticized Mary's unseemly public behavior, they were sharply rebuked. Christ made it clear that criticism of Mary was strictly off limits. Was it because her damaged soul was so fragile? Did Christ fear that the moral disapproval of her family and community would send Mary spiraling off course yet again? Or was it because Mary was the only one who understood that the only safe place on this earth is at the feet of the Master? (See Luke 10:38-42; John 12:1-7.)

THOUGHTS TO PONDER
- ❀ Have I accepted Christ's forgiveness for my own self-destructive choices, or do I still validate the criticism of my family and friends through the demons of shame and doubt?
- ❀ If Christ could rescue and forgive Mary Magdalene, certainly there is nothing in my life that Christ cannot heal. What do I desire to lay at the feet of the Master today?

"There is no real teacher who in practice does not believe in the existence of the soul, or in a magic that acts on it through speech."—Allan Bloom, American educator, 1930-1992

CONTINUING EDUCATION

Mary found an educational opportunity of a lifetime, sitting at the feet of Jesus. During Mary's day, religious training was considered a waste of time for women. Jesus disagreed and gave Mary the spiritual education and mentoring her soul longed for. Today, many women choose continuing-education opportunities to update their skills or explore new interests. Consider taking advantage of your company's ongoing education opportunities or explore some options on your own, such as a class at a local community center. If you are serious about continuing your education toward an advanced degree, you may wish to explore the American Association of University Women's Web site for information on grants and local chapters: <www.aauw.org>. Learning is a lifetime pursuit.

A Woman's Work

A woman's work involves a great deal of pain. Ask any woman in labor about Eve's curse, and she will probably curse Eve too. I thought I understood my tolerance for pain until I experienced childbirth. A friend of mine, describing the excruciating details of trying for hours to deliver a child that was attempting to enter the world shoulder first instead of head first, remarked, "At that point I truly believed that there was no possible outcome that could make this level of pain worth it. Then they laid my baby in my arms!" My friend's voice choked, and her eyes welled up with tears. It's a mystery. Of course it was worth it and much, much more! The pain is a pale comparison to the awesome wonder of new life in tiny toes, scrunchy eyes, and little wet lips. Don't get me wrong. I am not an advocate of pain as any sort of moral badge of courage. My motto is, "If pain can be avoided, do so immediately!" But as mothers, we have a perspective on pain that perhaps those who have not experienced childbirth do not. No matter how excruciating, it is worth it. It is a mystery.

Perhaps that is why God chose childbirth as a way to describe this sinful earth's passage into glory. Earth is wracked with pain. The pain of the innocent, the pain of the helpless, the pain of children—we sink under the staggering weight of pain in this life. We are experiencing the labor pains of salvation. Is there any possible outcome that could make this level of pain worth it? We lean into our faith. Someday this earth will emerge in glory. All tears will be wiped away, all pain vanquished, all sin revealed, all destruction destroyed. And this new birth, this new creation, will be ours, safe for eternity. Hallelujah! It's a mystery.

I consider that our present sufferings are not worth comparing with the glory that will be revealed in us (Romans 8:18).

We know that the whole creation has been groaning as in the pains of childbirth (Romans 8:22).

THOUGHTS TO PONDER
- What can I do to relieve pain and suffering in my small sphere?
- Have I ever experienced healing of pain in my life? Can I trust God to provide healing for the pain inflicted on this earth in the earth made new?

"Christ's grave was the birthplace of an indestructible belief that death is vanquished and there is life eternal."—Adolph Harnack

GIFTS FOR NEW MOTHER

Do you know a new mother? Baby showers are great in preparing for baby's needs, but new mothers have big needs to. Consider ways you can ease a young mother's postpartum stress. Your kindness will be cherished. Following are some ideas. I'm sure you can think of others.

- Deliver a casserole, a pot of homemade soup, or some other type of prepared food to help Mom make time for mealtime.
- Offer to make a grocery run for Mom.
- Have a fruit basket delivered.
- Mail a coupon for a free night of babysitting.
- Offer to take older siblings out for breakfast or to the park for a few hours.
- Send a gift certificate from a local laundry service.

Heart and Hand

Do what you love, and you will love what you do. Sounds like good advice, but how do you make that happen? Ralph Mattson and Arthur Miller, industrial psychologists and coauthors of the book *The Truth About You,* claim that if you consider your talents and skills with two important criteria in mind, you can uncover your primary motivation: what it is that makes you tick, what it is that makes hard work seem like play—in other words, the truth about you. The key is to identify things that you love to do *and* that you do really well.

When heart and hand are married, when passion and talent are merged, where love and discipline reside together, that is where you exist as your purest, most true self. A simple but brilliant idea. What do you do that you love doing and that you also do really well? Is it organizing, building, designing, helping others, bargain hunting, encouraging, teaching? What do you do even if you don't get paid to do it? If you do it well but don't love doing it, it's not the real thing. If you love doing it, but you are not very good at it, that doesn't count either. Heart and hand, passion and talent, we are fearfully and wonderfully made. God created us to do what we love, and He gifted us with the talents to support that passion. That is our unique contribution to life. Nobody else in the universe can play that role as well as we can. Mattson and Miller argue that a primary motivation never changes; in fact, we appear to be born with it. Peripheral skills and talents ebb and wane, but our primary motivations remain constant. Seek out those things you love and excel at. That is what you were created for. That is your greatest gift. When you do what you love, you will love what you do.

THOUGHTS TO PONDER

❀ Have I ever gotten caught in a rut because I can do something well but I don't have a passion for it?

❀ Do I have the courage to say No to the things that do not inspire me and Yes to the things that do?

BLACK BEAN PATTIES
VEGETARIAN ENTREE

These black bean patties can be served as an appetizer or as an entree. Preparation time: 25 minutes, 1 hour refrigeration. Cooking time: 20 minutes. Serves 12-15.

Pantry Items
Black beans (2 cans)
Olive oil (2 Tbsp.)
Pepper sauce (1 tsp.)
Cumin (1 tsp.)
Pepper (1 tsp.)
Seasoned bread crumbs (1 1/2 cup)
Cornmeal (2/3 cup)
Vegetable oil (1/2 cup)

Fresh Items
Onion (1/4 cup, chopped)
Bell pepper (1/4 cup, chopped)
Fresh garlic (4 cloves, diced)
Fresh parsley (3 sprigs, diced)
Eggs (2 yolks)

DIRECTIONS
Sauté chopped onion, bell pepper, and garlic in olive oil until tender. Drain and rinse black beans. Mix together beans, sauteéd vegetables, pepper sauce, parsley, cumin, pepper, egg yolks, and bread crumbs. Cover and chill 1 hour. Form mixture into 1/2-inch thick patties and coat with cornmeal. Heat vegetable oil over moderate heat. Fry patties in batches, about 1 1/2 minutes each side. Transfer to paper towels to drain. Reheats well in microwave if covered.

Pride and Prejudice

Pride and Prejudice, the popular Jane Austen novel, has never gone out of print since it was first published in 1813. There are a lot of good reasons for that bit of literary notoriety, but I think one of the most primal is that we are all so guilty. Who isn't afflicted with pride and prejudice? We certainly have to admit we have our pride. And if we are honest with ourselves, we all have our prejudices, as well. Like the characters in the book, we find that our pride and our prejudices do not serve us well. They trip us up; they deceive us; they keep us from the things that would make us happiest.

Not until God can dismantle our pride and break down our prejudices can He use us effectively. Just ask Moses or Jonah or Paul. I once had a fine Christian woman confess to me that she would never allow her husband to accept a call to a certain part of the country that she considered common and unsophisticated. I have learned not to make those demands on God. First, because I'm pretty sure that if I do, that's where I'm going next, and second, because I've learned that's probably where I'm going to want to be. There is no job too common, no place too humble, no lifestyle too simple to separate us from the love of God, the humor of God, or the joy of God. But our pride and our prejudice can do that in the nicest surroundings.

THOUGHTS TO PONDER
- ❀ Have I ever allowed my pride or my prejudices to keep me from following God?
- ❀ Do I trust God enough to allow Him to use me as He wills, not as I will?

SING-A-LONG WITH RHYTHM BAND
INSIDE OR OUTSIDE ACTIVITY

Ages: 5 to Adult
Materials Needed:
   Assorted household items (see below)

An old-fashioned rollicking sing-a-long in which everyone makes and
   plays an instrument. "Oh When the Saints, Come Marching In . . ."

Drums: Upside-down cooking pot, large empty can with lid, empty oatmeal box with lid.
Drumsticks: Pencils, chopsticks, wooden spoons. Try covering the ends of some drumsticks with
   padding (socks or yarn).
Rattles: Plastic jars with lids, baby-food jars with lids, empty cardboard roll with wax paper
   taped at both ends. Fill rattles with dried beans or popcorn kernels.
Kazoos: Wax paper taped over comb, wax paper attached to end of empty cardboard roll with
   rubber band.
Box Guitar: Slip rubber bands of varying sizes over a metal loaf pan or lidless shoebox.
Cymbals: Pan lids.
Bells: Car keys, jingle bells strung on shoelaces, empty tin cans. Pierce hole in top, thread yarn
   through hole, tie metal washer on inside, loop yarn on outside for handle.
Water Music: Drinking glasses, glass bottles. Fill glasses or bottles with various levels of water for
   different sounds and tap with drumstick.

Glass Ceilings

If you are a professional woman "of a certain age," you know all about glass ceilings. You undoubtedly received a nasty bruise or two from those invisible ceilings on your flight up the corporate ladder. If you are smart and if you were lucky, you may have even broken a few glass ceilings in your time. Congratulations! I wouldn't be surprised if you still have the embedded glass shards to prove it. Patronizing men with smirks and condescending tones of voice still make the hairs prickle on the back of my neck.

Young women today are less likely to encounter the invisible ceiling on their career paths. Executive and management positions are more accessible to women than they were a few years ago. The obstacle young women are encountering today is the wrath of the queen bees. For all our posturing about equality, it seems that once we forced our way into the good-old-boys' club, we turned around and slammed the door shut behind us. There is something pretty heady about being the only woman on the board of directors, the only woman in upper management, the only woman at the conference table. Shame on us! Give me patronizing men with smirks on their faces any day!

THOUGHTS TO PONDER
- ❀ Am I actively nurturing and mentoring my subordinates?
- ❀ Am I modeling Christlike management skills?

"The welfare of each is bound up in the welfare of all."
—*Helen Keller*

QUEEN BEES

Rosalind Wiseman's groundbreaking 2002 book, *Queen Bees and Wannabes,* pulls back the curtain on adolescent girls' cruel social pecking order. Wiseman writes, "Adolescence is a time when social hierarchies are powerfully and painfully reinforced every moment of every day." She has cofounded a nonprofit organization called "Empower" that has the motto "Violence should not be a rite of passage." How do we protect our daughters from being picked on, and how do we make sure they are not participating in mean-spirited behaviors toward other girls? Wiseman's research indicates that even the most difficult young women want their parents' advice and confidence. Her book offers several practical suggestions on ways you can help your daughter navigate her adolescence safely. Here are a few I'd like to add:

- ❀ Talk frankly with your daughter about social bullying and how damaging it is for both the one being bullied as well as the one doing the bullying.
- ❀ Listen carefully to what your daughter tells you and try to respond to her fears, not to your own painful memories.
- ❀ Refrain from trying to "fix" your daughter's social problems. Instead, try brainstorming with her on ways she can deal with her problems.
- ❀ Even though it may seem poor comfort, assure your daughter that "this too will pass," and as she moves on toward college and adulthood, social bullying will subside.
- ❀ Assure her that you love her and you will always be in her corner no matter how tough the going gets.

Driving Force

What drives you to excel? What fuels your accomplishments? Is it passion or pride or desire to provide for your family? Whether we are career women or homemakers, we have an innate desire to do what we do well. There is no shame in our choices if we accept no shame. Women who chose to stay home and women who chose to pursue a career are equally vulnerable to criticism. Regardless of which choice we make, we are often tempted to accept the guilt and criticisms that come with our choices. Isn't it time for us to refuse to do that and focus our energy on the reasons we made our choice in the first place—our families, our talents, our quality of life? Whatever we do, it is worthy of being done well, and we can't do that if we are constantly conflicted. It diminishes our actions if we are not free to perform them with pride and dignity. So I'll ask again, What is your driving force? Whatever it is, celebrate it, enjoy it, rejoice in it, and thank God for it!

Whatever your hand finds to do, do it with all your might (Ecclesiastes 9:10).

THOUGHTS TO PONDER
- Do I seriously need to rethink my life choices, or do I need to ignore the cacophony of criticism?
- Do the life choices that I have made resonate honestly with the woman I desire to be?

"What is work and what is not work are questions that perplex the wisest of men."
—*Bhagavad Gita*

PASSIONS

Is there something that you are passionate about? Do you have a hobby or an interest that ignites your enthusiasm? Have you considered pursuing your passion professionally? Many women develop fulfilling careers out of their passions and interests. Other women prefer keeping them as part-time hobbies and avocations they can enjoy without the pressures of financial feasibility. There is no one answer that is correct for all women. To help you determine what might work best for you, thoughtfully consider the following questions:

❀ Would I enjoy pursuing my interest or hobby full-time, or do I prefer using my interest or hobby as a means to add depth and quality to my life?
❀ Does my interest or hobby have income-producing potential? Is the potential income sufficient to justify making it a full-time endeavor, or is it more suited to supplementary income?

If you think that you might like to explore full-time options, here are a few suggestions to get you started:

❀ Talk to someone who has built a successful business in your field of interest.
❀ Locate professional associations or trade groups in your area that can help you get inside industry know-how, seminars, and contacts.
❀ Develop a twelve-month cash-flow plan, outlining your expected expenses and income. Review your plan with a qualified individual such as a small business administration counselor.
❀ Find a good accountant who is experienced with small businesses to make sure you are set up to keep good records and comply with all government regulations that might apply to your business. (This is the most important step you will take!)
❀ Treat your new business with the same respect you would any job. Keep regular hours, faithfully return business phone calls, and maintain your business records.
GOOD LUCK!

If Wishes Were Horses

"If wishes were horses, beggars would ride," my great-grandmother was fond of saying. And my great-grandmother knew a thing or two about horses. She learned to ride bareback with the boys in the old country. My great-grandmother knew a thing or two about wishes as well. She arrived at Ellis Island as a young teenage girl with her widowed mother. Robbed of all their possessions just before boarding the ship bound for New York, the two women landed penniless, with nothing but the clothes on their backs. Somehow they survived, even thrived. There was no shortage of jobs in the sweatshops. Young Elizabeth attracted the attention of a handsome young immigrant. His family was setting him up with a real American business, a bottling factory in New Jersey. Their wedding was a huge community affair with seventeen bridesmaids and groomsmen. Soon they built a beautiful American house, and Elizabeth bore three sons. It seemed that in America wishes did indeed come true.

But that was not the end of the story. On the brink of the Great Depression, my great-grandfather died suddenly in an accident. Elizabeth was left to care for three young boys and an elderly mother as the bottom fell out of the economy. A young, uneducated woman should have lost everything, but she didn't. She sold the business but kept the land. She returned to work in the sweatshops; she took on borders. She kept her sons together and out of the gangs that flourished during Prohibition. "If wishes were horses, beggars would ride." Elizabeth never looked back. As the Depression dragged on, she managed to feed her family as well as a string of hobos who rode the trains that ran by her door. Her house was marked in the hobo sign for "kind woman lives here." My great-grandmother passed away in 1970. For several years after her death, strangers continued to stop by the house to pay respects to the "kind woman" who had lived there. Nobody had any idea of how many families Elizabeth had supported through the years with clothing, food, and money both in this country and the old country. "If wishes were horses, beggars would ride." Elizabeth saw to it that wishes did indeed become horses. When life gives me less than I'd hoped for, I picture a young girl on a horse racing across the Hungarian steppe, hair and skirts flying behind her. "If wishes were horses, beggars would ride."

THOUGHT TO PONDER
❀ How do I cope with adversity and hard times?

"When our eyes see our hands doing the work of our hearts, the circle of Creation is completed inside us, the doors of our souls fly open and love steps forth to heal everything in sight."
—*Michael Bridge*

MY HERITAGE

Are there women in your family who have accomplished amazing things or lived amazing lives? You will want to preserve this legacy to pass down to your daughters. Embark on a quest to learn more about your "fore-mothers." Consider ways you can share your family's history of great women:

- ❀ Create a scrapbook of old photographs, letters, and documents.
- ❀ Compile a keepsake box of treasured letters and personal items.
- ❀ Write down their story and illustrate with old photographs.
- ❀ Build a shadow-box display with their picture, historical documents, and items that will encourage questions about the women featured.

Labor of Love

Before you have children of your own, you really don't notice other people's children except in passing. A few weeks after the birth of my first child, I found myself sitting in the back of a fellowship hall quietly feeding my newborn. Another mother at the church potluck caught my attention as I observed her tending to a toddler and an infant. It was like watching a complex choreographed ballet. First she changed diapers, set up portable child seats, and attached and reattached bibs. Then she pulled out a series of little jars for the infant and a container of Cheerios for the impatient four-year-old. She wiped up spills and soothed the baby while trying to keep the toddler occupied with an endless string of books and toys pulled from the diaper bag. By the time Dad returned, balancing three plates of food, I couldn't help letting out a sigh of relief. Finally Mom could relax and enjoy her meal.

But then the real fun began. The four-year-old immediately disqualified most of her father's culinary choices. The only acceptable choices required cutting and buttering while Mom simultaneously executed a series of body blocks to keep the now cranky infant from snatching his sister's food. I could tell she was losing the battle. Yellow sticky stuff, squash or apricots, had spread over the baby like a bad rash on hands, mouth, hair, clothes. Swipes of it were appearing on Mom and sister. It didn't look good. The pile of wet wipes continued to grow on the table, but the children didn't seem much improved. Finally I could take the suspense no longer. I leaned toward the exhausted mom whose own plate of food had not yet been touched. "How long until they can eat on their own?" I asked, desperate to know the answer as my mind calculated days, minutes, and hours in a wild panic. The young mother looked at me for a few moments before replying. I could sense the same wild calculations running through her mind. "I don't know," she finally answered as she deftly fielded a sippy cup in flight.

THOUGHTS TO PONDER
- New mothers have a grueling, 24/7 labor of love. What does my church do to support and help new mothers?
- Is there something I might do to lighten the load of a new mother in my church or community?

"The labor of keeping house is labor in its most naked state, for labor is toil that never finishes, toil that has to be begun again the moment it is completed, toil that is destroyed and consumed by the life process." —Mary Mccarthy, American author, 1912-1989

MINISTRY FOR NEW MOMS

Ministering to new moms is a rich avenue of service often overlooked by the church. With the fragmentation in our mobile society, new moms are often left to struggle the best they can on their own without the traditional support of extended family. There are so many ways a church can help. Here are a few ideas that have worked for some groups. What can your group do?

- ❀ Give a gift basket from the church to all new moms, distributed at local hospitals.
- ❀ Offer church-sponsored classes for new moms and moms to be.
- ❀ Offer once-a-week childcare at the church while moms attend classes or Bible study.
- ❀ Purchase supplemental food and baby clothing for underprivileged moms.
- ❀ Hold community Sabbath School for un-churched moms and kids.
- ❀ Offer in-home new-baby instruction for first-time moms, coordinated through a local agency.

Workaholics

Workaholic. It sounds like such an admirable addiction, doesn't it? Favorite interview response to the interviewer's question, "Mrs. Smith, what would you say is your greatest weakness?"

"Well, Ms. Hot Shot Executive with no family, I guess I have to confess that I'm a bit of a workaholic. I work late most evenings and often come in on weekends." That response might get you the job, but it certainly won't get you a life. Workaholics, like all addicts, start out thinking they are the ones in control; but like all addicts, they eventually discover that they are willing to pay just about any price for the all-important high. It doesn't matter whether you're tripping on power or cocaine or even stress, for that matter, if the end result is that you're sacrificing your health and your family to support your habit. Depression, exhaustion, and insomnia are the formidable companions to addiction. It doesn't help your home life if you are happy only when you're working.

Power, stress, and fierce competition are strong emotions, pumping high doses of adrenalin into our bloodstreams. It's the fight-or-flight response and was never intended to be a lifestyle. We can become addicted to our own power surge. After prolonged exposure, we no longer feel like ourselves unless we can experience the adrenalin surging through our systems. As any Alcoholics Anonomous veteran will tell you, admitting a problem is the first step on the path to recovery. "Hello, my name is Patricia, and I am a workaholic."

THOUGHTS TO PONDER

❋ Am I able to leave my work at the office, or do I find it habitually impacting my personal life?

❋ If I am not spending as much time with my family as I would like, what steps can I take to change my lifestyle?

"In order that people may be happy in their work, these three things are needed: They must be fit for it: they must not do too much of it: and they must have a sense of success in it."
—W. H. Auden, poet 1907-1973

SOFT ADDICTIONS

"Soft Addictions" are destructive, repetitive habits that are not tied to a direct chemical or physical addiction, such as nicotine, drugs, or alcohol. Recovering from even so-called soft addictions can be a challenging process. Psychologists and counselors are recognizing and treating the destructive habits of otherwise addiction-free adults. How do you know whether your behavior is just your way of relaxing or whether it falls into the soft-addiction category? Here are a few telltale signs:

- Is your repetitive behavior interfering with your family relationships, such as spending hours every day surfing the Internet, playing games, or talking on the phone?
- Does your habit interfere with your work, such as constantly stopping to check Internet news updates, stock quotes, or email?
- Is your habit affecting your health, such as an addiction to sweets, constant snacking, or staying up late every night watching TV?
- Is your behavior taxing your finances, such as compulsive collecting, online shopping, or daily purchases from TV shopping channels?

If you suspect that your behavior is out of control, you may want to seek the assistance of a professional counselor or get some more information by reading a book dealing with compulsive behaviors. Two recommended books on the topic are *The Heart of Addiction* by Dr. Lance Dodes or *Breaking the Pattern* by Charles Platkin.

Balancing Acts

I like the medieval concept of God as the perfect circle, all elements in balance—love/justice, power/humility, activity/repose. God embodies perfection. He has no deficiencies. Sin is inherently a distortion, an overindulgence of one thing, a lack of another. Sin is all work and no play, or all play with no responsibility. Sin is mercy without justice or vice versa. Sin is sex without commitment. And sometimes sin is a cold, passionless marriage. God made us multifaceted creatures. We were created to live life in balance, partaking of all God's gifts and abusing none of them. But, unfortunately, Eve believed the serpent's lie, "Eat, and ye shall be as gods" (see Genesis 3:4), implying, perhaps, that we could make up our own rules and not suffer the consequences. But we cannot recreate the universe. Living unbalanced lives is like trying to spin an unbalanced top. We only wobble and topple, and if we exert enormous effort, we careen wildly across the floor and crash into the wall. Unbalanced tops never achieve the momentum to spin productively within their sphere.

THOUGHTS TO PONDER
- What aspects of my life need balance?
- How would my life change if I were to consciously strive for a healthy balance?

FRESH STRAWBERRY DESSERT
SUMMER DESSERT

This deceptively easy summer dessert calls for fresh strawberries (although you can substitute frozen) that will garner you a peck of compliments. Preparation time: 20 minutes. Baking time: 10 minutes. Refrigerate: 4 hours or overnight. Serves 10-12.

Pantry Items
Pretzels (2 2/3 cups, crushed coarsely)
Sugar (1 cup + 3 Tbsp.)
Strawberry gelatin (1 6-oz. box)

Fresh Items
Strawberries (1 pint)
Butter or margarine (3/4 cup, softened)
Cream cheese (1 8-oz. package, softened)
Nondairy whipped topping (4-oz. carton)

DIRECTIONS
Preheat oven to 350° F. Trim and slice fresh strawberries. Bring kettle of water to boil. Pour gelatin into a large bowl. Pour 2 cups of boiling water over gelatin. Mix until dissolved. Stir in strawberries and refrigerate until partially set. In a medium bowl, cream softened butter or margarine with 3 tablespoons of sugar. Mix in crushed pretzels. Press pretzel mixture evenly into the bottom of a 9" x 13" glass casserole dish. Bake for 10 minutes. Remove from oven and cool. Meanwhile, cream together softened cream cheese and 1 cup of sugar. Gently fold nondairy whipped topping into cream cheese mixture. Spread cream cheese mixture evenly over cooled crust. Pour partially set strawberry gelatin over cream cheese and smooth. (If gelatin mixture isn't set enough, it will cause a soggy crust.) Cover with plastic wrap and refrigerate 4 hours or overnight.

SERVING SUGGESTIONS
Cut into squares. Add a dollop of whipped topping and garnish with a fresh strawberry.

Mothers and Daughters

Have you ever considered what type of woman you are modeling for your daughter—or, for that matter, for your son? Our children absorb our norms much more readily than they do our ideals. I remember the mild shock of hearing my six-year-old son proudly declare, "When I grow up and get married, I'm going to cook great meals for my wife, just like dad does." I knew I had been working late a lot recently. But it took me a few moments to admit that I rarely arrived home in time to start supper and maybe that situation had been going on for longer than just "recently."

There is nothing wrong with a father who cooks great meals. There may be something wrong if a mother never has the time to. On the other hand, a mother who always cooks and cleans up after everyone else might not be the model we want our sons and daughters to absorb as normal either. It's a brave new world out there. Many women work outside the home. Some men are choosing to work at home. The way we live out our choices on a day-to-day basis will impact our children and their relationships and possibly even their children. Don't we owe it to them to model lifestyles based on dignity, respect, and personal responsibility for each member of the family?

THOUGHT TO PONDER

❀ Is the woman I think I should be really the type of woman I want to model for my daughter?

"More men are killed by overwork than the importance of the world justifies."
—Rudyard Kipling, poet, 1865-1936

MOSS GARDENS
OUTSIDE ACTIVITY

Ages: 5 to 12
Materials Needed:
   Pie plate for each child (disposable ones are fine)
   Nature items collected from a walk, such as moss, pine cones, pebbles,
      shells, twigs
   Small plastic animals
   Play-Doh modeling compound (optional)

One of my favorite childhood memories is walking with my grandmother to the creek on a crisp autumn afternoon. With a battered pie plate in hand for each of her grandchildren, she would sit on the bank while we collected moss, pebbles, little sticks, feathers, and colorful leaves. She would ohh and ahh over each treasure and pile them up in neat little piles next to her knees. When the treasure hunt was over, we would sit in a semicircle around her, arranging our treasures into miniature landscapes in our pie plates. Grandma would oversee our efforts like an architect, praising and critiquing in turn. When we were finished, we would carefully carry our projects back to her kitchen, and she would add a "lake" to each landscape by pouring water from her measuring cup into the little hole we carefully left in the center of each landscape.

This is a great Sabbath-afternoon activity for children of almost all ages. The littlest ones can participate, and even the older ones seem to find it irresistible. A bag of little plastic animals turns the landscape into the Garden of Eden, heaven, or Noah's ark. If no moss is available in your area, Play-Doh is a good substitute.

Sisterhood

Women's roles in society as well as in the church have been challenged and expanded over the past few years, or so it seems to us with only a hundred years or so of personal memory gleaned through our mothers and grandmothers. The rest is just history. The controversial fact remains that feminism has impacted the lives of Christian women, as it has all women in our society. We have more choices. We have fewer role models. We have conflicting expectations. Bottom line, we are suffering from more guilt. No matter what choices we make, we must leave some expectations unfulfilled. We will always be subject to criticism. There is no one-size-fits-all pattern. Even the Bible is clear on that. God has called women to be prophets, mothers, wives, warriors, rulers, merchants, beauty queens, and spies.

God reserves the right to use us as He sees fit. Why should we reserve the right to criticize one another? We all belong to the same sisterhood. Every woman, whether she works in the home or in the marketplace, can do so to the glory of God. Every woman, whether she is an executive or a homemaker, can live a selfish, egocentric life. The difference is not in the profession; the difference is in the heart. We are a sisterhood of believers. Our calling is to nurture and encourage one another. We must bear one another's burdens. We must affirm one another's calling. In short, we must value one another because we are valued in Christ. We are a sisterhood.

THOUGHTS TO PONDER

- ❀ Am I ever tempted to criticize women who have made lifestyle choices different from my own?
- ❀ In what practical ways can I affirm and support women in my church who are not like me?

"Let us rise in the moral power of womanhood; and give utterance to the voice of outraged mercy, and insulted justice, and eternal truth, and mighty love and holy freedom."
—Maria Weston Chapman

CUTTING GARDENS

Cutting gardens are one of life's true luxuries, a luxury that busy women believe they don't have the time to indulge in. Fortunately, several hardy cutting-flower varieties require little upkeep. Fresh flowers add a warm and beautiful touch to a home that no other decorative touch can. Fresh flowers are one of the most cherished gifts a woman can bestow upon a friend or neighbor. Following are some tips and suggestions for growing and giving beautiful flowers:

- ❀ **Popular Cutting Perennials:** Roses, black-eyed Susans, carnations, yarrow, peonies, and iris.
- ❀ **Popular Cutting Annuals:** Marigolds, sunflowers, zinnias, sweet peas, gladiolus, larkspur.
- ❀ **Conditioning Cut Flowers:** Conditioning prepares cut flowers to stay fresh for as long as possible. Whether you pick flowers fresh from your garden or purchase them from the florist, the following simple procedure will extend the life of your cut blooms:

  1. You can purchase a commercial floral solution, or you can mix your own. For every quart of water, add 2 aspirin to help stems absorb water, 1 teaspoon of sugar to nourish the flowers, and a drop or two of bleach to reduce bacteria.
  2. Remove dead leaves or leaves that will rest below the waterline. Make a sharp, clean diagonal cut near the end of the stem and immerse immediately in floral solution. A diagonal cut prevents stems from sitting flat on the bottom of a vase, unable to absorb water.
  3. If flowers are fresh, allow the stems to condition in the floral solution for two to three hours before arranging in vases filled with fresh solution.

United We Stand

It doesn't matter where or how we spend our working hours. As women, we all face the same challenges. How do we rear our children to be responsible, caring adults? How do we keep our marriages vibrant and alive? How do we make sound financial decisions? How do we find time for our families and still make a contribution to our churches and our communities? There are no easy answers. There are only hard choices. But it helps if we have a network of support. Many Americans feel increasingly isolated and separated from their families. We have become a nation of nomads. According the U.S. Census Bureau, approximately 43 million Americans are on the move from one place to another each year. Our support systems have broken down. Our family units have disintegrated. It's no wonder that many women feel cut off and alone. As Christian women, we have a place to turn to for support—or at least I think that's what Christ intended. Too often, I'm afraid, we find censor and disapproval in our church communities instead of help and encouragement. In our rush to fix one another's problems, we may forget that a sympathetic ear is sometimes the most critical need and the greatest encouragement. Real women have real problems. None of us is exempt from the heartaches and heartbreaks of this world. If we have the courage to admit that we don't have all the answers, perhaps it will give our sisters the encouragement they need to express their hopes and fears. We all need a safe place to share our concerns. What a tender ministry we can perform for one another. United we stand, divided we perish.

THOUGHTS TO PONDER
- Do I have a safe place to discuss my hopes and concerns?
- Can I be a safe place for someone I know to share her dreams and heartaches?

"I've always thought that people need to feel good about themselves and I see my role as offering support to them, to provide some light along the way."—Princess Diana

TENDER AFFIRMATIONS

One of the most emotionally taxing jobs I've ever held was working as a church secretary. Church secretaries absorb the impact of the congregation's spiritual frustrations. And apparently our frustrations are many. After a particularly assaulting day, a coworker commented that mine was a thankless job. I replied, somewhat bitterly, that I would be so delighted if my job ever were elevated to merely thankless. Surprisingly, we as Christians are quick to criticize and slow to praise. We seem to readily notice the speck in our sister's eye and completely miss the burdens on her shoulders. What if it were the other way around? What if we ignored the smeared mascara and offered a shoulder instead: a shoulder to lean on, a shoulder to cry on, a shoulder to share the burdens? Is there a woman in your congregation who could benefit from tender affirmation this week?

❀ Send a note of appreciation to a faithful worker in your church.
❀ Notice something nice about a single mom's children this week and tell her what it is.
❀ Invite a recently widowed or single woman out to lunch.
❀ Compliment the deaconesses on the beautiful flowers.
❀ Prepare a small gift and thank-you card for your child's Sabbath School teacher.
❀ Bring a long-stemmed rose in a vase for the organist.
❀ Tell the church secretary that the bulletin looks great!

Divided We Fall

She was everything a fine Christian woman should be, and her church admired her unreservedly. She was asked to serve in a variety of positions, including church elder, Sabbath School superintendent, and discipleship coordinator. Several times a year she was invited to present the Sabbath sermon. She had a lovely smile. Her simple, tailored suits enhanced her dignity and authority. But what she kept scrupulously concealed from her church began to take its toll on her. A certain rigidity, an unattractive critical spirit began to permeate her interactions. There were no big confrontations. She was too refined for that, but even her closest relationships within the church grew increasingly estranged. When nominating committee rolled around at the end of the year, she resigned all her positions and refused to serve in any capacity. The church was dumbfounded and confused. I was a little piqued myself, since the church was not that large, and the responsibilities were many.

In a quiet conversation one Sabbath morning, I implored her directly to help out at least a little. I was not prepared for the flood of bitter confessions that poured from her soul.

An abusive, drug-addicted adult son had left her financially ruined, destitute, and facing an enormous lawsuit. Her burdens were overwhelming. Tears welled in my eyes as I knelt to pray with her. But before we could pray, she swore me to secrecy. "Of course," I replied, "but your church family loves you, and certainly you could talk to the pastor or to some of your friends. We care about you." She was adamant that absolutely nobody was to know about her problems. She had brought her son's addiction to the church once before and had reported how God had healed him. She was determined not to let the church know that her son had relapsed and what he had done to her. She observed bitterly that no one in the church cared about her. "But how can they care if you don't let them know?" I asked. She was too distressed to recognize the irony of her statement. As she prayed, she implored God earnestly to convict the congregation of their sins. It seemed a strange prayer under the circumstances. She left with her head held high and her church smile firmly in place.

United we stand; divided and isolated we will certainly perish.

THOUGHTS TO PONDER
- ❀ Am I guilty of constructing a facade to keep my church family at arm's length?
- ❀ If I were to be more open with my church family about my hopes and heartaches, what would happen?

"Pleasure can be supported by an illusion; but happiness rests upon truth."
—Sebastien-Roch Nicolas De Chamfort, 1741-1794

A GENUINE WOMAN

Women receive admonition from a wide spectrum of experts, ranging from spiritual leaders to self-help gurus, to "Get Real!" But how does one do that without coming across as bitter, negative, or needy? Perhaps it's by remembering who we really are. Here are a few thoughts:

❀ I am a Forgiven Sinner Woman—I don't need to hide my past.
❀ I am a Forgiven Sinner Woman—I don't need to cover my faults.
❀ I am a Forgiven Sinner Woman—I don't need to pretend I don't have problems.
❀ I am a Forgiven Sinner Woman—I don't need to put down my sister for her faults.
❀ I am a Forgiven Sinner Woman—I don't need to be happy all the time, but I can be grateful all the day long for being a Forgiven Sinner Woman.

Life in the Fast Lane

"Eat of the fruit and ye shall be as gods," the serpent lied to Eve. Experiencing everything, all the time—the original lie, the great illusion. But we are not gods. We are merely the children of God. For us is appointed a time and season. Can women have it all—a career, a marriage, a family? I have always hated that question. I believe the answer is Yes, but everything, all the time is certainly fatal. Every pinnacle in life cannot be compressed into one moment without a hefty bill. The right house, cars, vacations, friends, clothes, schools, promotions—what does it cost to have it all right now, in one bright, shiny bundle? What are we willing to sacrifice? our health? our children? our marriages? our careers? Obviously we don't want to sacrifice any of those things. So we are left with choices. To everything there is a time and a season. Life is longer than we think. Life is shorter than we think. What do we really want out of it? We have some choices to make. We were never created to survive life in the fast lane.

THOUGHTS TO PONDER
- Has my life accelerated out of control? Am I moving too fast to see the stop signs?
- What steps can I take today to restore a healthy balance to my life?

"Character is the sum and total of a person's choices."
—P. B. Fitzwater

GET A LIFE

All work and no play makes for a very long day! Why are we working so hard? Does it make sense? Is it because we need to or because we *need* to? We all go through particularly busy times in our lives, but if we're feeling rushed and out of control 70 percent of the time or more, we're not doing a very good job managing our lives. We're smart girls, and certainly we can figure out a way to live the kind of lives we want to. Make your own life plan. Plan life the way you would like it to be. Why not?

1. List the things you need to do every week.
2. List the things you want to do every week.
3. Purchase, make, or go online for a good weekly calendar.
4. Set up your week the way you want to. Schedule the things you need to do **and** the things you want to do.
5. Life is about choices. You may have to delegate some "need to do's" to make sure you retain some "want to do's." You may need to rethink some of your responsibilities. You may have to exercise your right to say No. What's wrong with that?

Life is about choices. Isn't it time you chose to have a life?

Wonder Woman and Other Myths

Wonder Woman doesn't exist, but if you were to check our to-do lists, you might be tempted to think that we believe she does. In my experience, it doesn't seem to matter whether women work inside or outside the home, we overschedule. Why do we find it so hard to say No? And we don't seem to be much better at asking for help. We labor under the delusion that everything depends on us. Who do we think we are, Wonder Woman? It's our job to see to it that the children are fed, the laundry is done, the floors are cleaned, the curtains are hung, the dog is groomed. Really? When did all that become our responsibility? If it's because we are the ones with the most time and the rest of the family is pitching in taking care of the lawn, the garbage, the minor repairs, and the car maintenance, then it makes sense, doesn't it? Every family should work out the basic stuff in a more or less equitable arrangement. Anything less than that just isn't fair. And if it isn't fair, someone is being taken advantage of. If we're taking advantage of our family, shame on us. It's time we grew up and pulled our own weight. If we're the ones allowing our family to take advantage of us, shame on us still. It's time they grew up and pulled their own weight.

The last thing our family needs is a mother martyr. Martyrs tend to adopt unpleasant, shrewish attitudes. There's no advantage in being one. We are women; as wonderful as that is, we still aren't Wonder Woman. We need to let go of our super-power myths and all the imaginary clout that goes along with it. We must learn to say No. We must learn to ask (nicely) for help. We must learn to help our family function as fully responsible members of a very important team. Now there's a myth worth questing for.

THOUGHTS TO PONDER
- ❀ How does my family divvy up the basic household duties? Does it make sense?
- ❀ If I say No to something I really don't want to do or don't have time for, do I feel guilty? Why?

"There are two primary choices in life: to accept conditions as they exist, or accept the responsibility for changing them."—Denis Waitley

CHILDHOOD CHORES

Some families pay allowances based on the performance of chores. Some families believe that doing chores is part of the price you pay for the privilege of belonging to a family. Either way, it can be a real chore to get kids to do their chores. Often it seems it would just be easier to do the chores yourself. But that is not really an option if we want to rear responsible human beings. Doing chores is a valuable character-building process for children. Next time you are tempted to let chores slip in exchange for a little peace and quiet, consider the following benefits your kids might be missing:

- Household chores lay the foundation of your children's future work ethic. Their future success will be affected by the work ethic they develop today.
- Chores build skills in concentration, attention to detail, and thoroughness—skills vital to academic or professional excellence.
- Chores build discipline. Doing the hard stuff before the fun stuff every day allows children to exercise their developing skills in discipline. Discipline gives them the ability to make things happen.
- Chores build self-respect in ways that verbal praise cannot. Doing important household chores well and faithfully builds a well of self-respect in your children that they can call on.

Secret Sisters

Secret Sisters is a favorite activity of women's groups. The object of the activity is to pick a name out of a hat and adopt that woman as a secret sister for the remainder of the year, remembering her birthday, anniversary, and other special days with little gifts and cards. Sometimes secret sisters leave presents for no reason at all or to congratulate or support their sister at certain momentous events in their lives. It's wonderfully fun. I have been blessed with award-winning secret sisters who have supported me with little notes, quotations, flowers, and thoughtful gifts for a full year. Unfortunately, I wish I were better at it. I tend to start out well, but as the year rolls on, my secret sister slips to the back of my mind. One day I realize with a start that I am way delinquent and begin searching desperately among the powders and perfumes in the drugstore for something meaningful.

I should probably stop drawing names, but the idea is so good! We need one another's support. We crave a little attention. We can live a week on a little note of encouragement or congratulation. I heard of a woman who buys vases at flea markets and fills one each week with flowers from her garden and presents it with a beautiful bow to a different woman at church each week. What a terrific idea! Wouldn't you just love to be a recipient of a gift like that? I heard of another woman who carries a "pizza pack" to church each week as a surprise gift. The pack consists of homemade pizza dough, a jar of sauce, and zip-lock bags of cheese and toppings. WOW! What can I say? These women are heroes of mine. I know of another woman who believes she has the gift of discernment and writes letters each week to unsuspecting church members, explaining their shortcomings and offering her prayers. There's really no contest on which kind of gift I'd rather receive. What about you?

THOUGHTS TO PONDER
❀ What is one of the nicest, most unexpected things another woman has done for me?
❀ Whom do I know that could really use a special surprise this week?

ZUCCHINI CASSEROLE
SEASONAL PRODUCE

This tasty entree goes together in a flash. Preparation time: 15 minutes. Baking time: 30-35 minutes. Serves 8. Doubles easily. Reheats well for potluck meals.

Pantry Items
Bisquick baking mix (1 cup)
Oil (1/2 cup)
Salt (1 tsp.)

Fresh Items
Zucchini (3 cups, diced)
Onion (1)
Fresh parsley (1/4 cup, chopped)
Parmesan cheese (1/2cup)
Cheddar cheese (1/2 cup)
Eggs (4))

DIRECTIONS
Rinse zucchini and dice (no need to peel). Finely chop onion and parsley. Pour vegetables into large mixing bowl. Mix in baking mix, Parmesan cheese, cheddar cheese, and salt. Whisk eggs and oil together in small bowl. Pour eggs over zucchini mixture and mix gently but thoroughly. Pour into 8" x 10" glass casserole dish. May be covered and refrigerated overnight. Bring to room temperature and remove cover before baking in a 350° F oven until golden brown, about 30 to 35 minutes.

Gossip, the Game

Have you ever played the game Gossip at a party? One person sitting in a large circle whispers a small tidbit of information to the individual sitting to their left. That person passes on the information to the individual on their left, and so on and so on, until the message travels the full circle and reaches the originator again. The difference between the original comment and the final retelling is usually significant and very funny—but only if it's just a party game.

In real life, gossip is a cruel game that inflicts real damage and lifelong scars. It has no place in Christian fellowship or ministry, and yet it is practiced on almost every occasion at which two or more are gathered together. Damage could be avoided if we followed the advice of a wise grandfather: Never open your mouth to talk about your friends until you have considered at least three things: (1) Is it kind? (2) Is it true? (3) Is it worth telling?

Imagine what Christian fellowship would be like if we allowed Grandfather's advice to monitor our conversations. It sounds like heaven to me.

THOUGHTS TO PONDER

❀ Am I ever tempted to share more than I should about another person's difficulties?

❀ Why am I tempted to indulge in such mean-spirited activity? How can I replace criticism with Christian charity in my conversations?

MIRACLE PLAY
INSIDE OR OUTSIDE ACTIVITY

Ages: 5 to Adult
Materials Needed:
  Costume material
  Fabric scraps
  Old sheets or towels
  Scarves and/or belts

During the medieval era, Mystery Plays or Miracle Plays were performed by traveling players or local villagers to illustrate biblical stories. Let your children select one or two stories of biblical miracles to enact in your own backyard Miracle Play. Ahead of time, prepare a box of fabric scraps, old sheets, towels, scarves, belts, etc. for improvised costumes. Your children will enjoy assigning parts, costuming, and locating props for the production. You can play along or be the audience. This is a fun activity for a small group of children. You may want to invite a few friends over.

Fearless

What are you afraid of—spiders, heights, dark nights, loneliness, failure, disappointment? For anyone who has suffered a full-blown, chest-pounding, breath-stopping anxiety attack, fear is no small matter, even if it is "only" generalized fear. Christ understands. "I would gather you under My wings as a hen gathers her chicks," He whispers with tears in His eyes. "I see the sparrow fall; I count the hairs on your head." He gently tries to reassure and calm us: "Fear not. Let not your heart be troubled." But He does not, cannot, promise us the safety we want. He will only promise us safety for eternity, safety from the clutches of the evil one.

We are not safe in this world. We will suffer illness, heartache, pain, and death. We will lose loved ones. We will walk through the shadow of death. But we will not face the great unknown alone, for we are known. With our hand in His, He will not allow evil to separate us from His love. Now we are earthbound and can see only the passing dangers, not the real evils. We cannot see the malice that wishes to abort our passage into eternity. He has opened that passage by His blood, and He would guard that passage with a thousand angels if need be. The children of God will not suffer irreparable harm. Temporal danger is the illusion of this earth, for we are safe for eternity. We will outlive fear by five million years and counting. He invites us to lean into His grace. Rest in His peace. This life with all its sorrows is but a moment in time. (See Matthew 10 and 23; John 14.)

I have told you these things, so that in me you may have peace. In this world you will have trouble. But take heart! I have overcome the world (John 16:33).

THOUGHTS TO PONDER

❀ Have I ever stopped to consider how short 100 years will seem against the backdrop of eternity?

❀ Can I imagine what it would be like to live and love in a universe without evil?

"Prosperity is not without many fears and distastes; adversity not without comforts and hopes."—Francis Bacon, British essayist, statesman, 1561-1626

GARDEN ROOMS

The term *garden room* sounds like a contradiction. However, the concept has gained popularity recently. As we have become increasingly urban and suburban, there remains a part of us that strongly desires to stay connected to nature. On limited suburban plots, garden rooms are a way to experience a variety of landscapes in compact spaces. By subdividing the garden into different focus areas and adding a few benches, swings, or seating areas, we can make our gardens an oasis for meditation and quiet chats. Here are some easy to construct garden rooms:

Butterfly Garden. Dedicate a quiet nook of the garden to plants and flowers attractive to butterflies, such as asters, marigolds, phlox, and butterfly weed. Add a comfy bench to curl up on, and your butterfly garden will provide hours of relaxing observation.

Rock Garden. My great-grandmother adored her rock garden. She planted bulbs between the rocks. Crocus and hyacinth bloomed in early spring while the rest of the garden was still barren. The rock garden was a little promise of spring. Later in the season, other bulbs would bloom, daffodil, tulips, iris, and finally day lilies and tiger lilies.

Hummingbird Garden. Pick a corner of the garden where plants can climb on a wall or trellis. Hummingbirds enjoy honeysuckle, delphiniums, columbine, petunias, phlox, and bee balm. Add a hummingbird feeder to attract the tiny birds, and they will make your garden a regular stop.

Dancing as Fast as I Can

Barbara Gordon was an award-winning documentary filmmaker. She was successful in a man's world and was widely respected and admired. Few people would have guessed that the sophisticated, world-traveling filmmaker suffered from near-crippling anxiety attacks. In her book, *I'm Dancing as Fast as I Can,* she relates her struggles first with depression and anxiety and then with severe Valium addiction. Pills became her lifeline and then her prison. Desperate to break free, Barbara tried going "cold turkey." Instead of releasing her, the attempt pushes her over the edge into a full-blown psychotic break, and she loses everything—her job, her reputation, her lover. In the hospital she works with a therapist on the difficult task of starting over. Rebuilding her life from the ground up. Barbara is one of the lucky ones; she survives. The message in her book: Pills are not a shortcut. They can suppress our anxieties, but they cannot make them go away. Sooner or later we have to deal with them.

Many women struggle with the combined pressures of work, family, and unreasonable expectations. It is tempting to take a little something to make it through the day, to sleep through the night. A little pick-me-up to get going, a little something to relax. It's easy to miss the obvious: Our life is not working; we need to make some changes. As frightening as that thought is, it's a good starting place.

THOUGHTS TO PONDER

❀ Do I ever feel overwhelmed and trapped by my life? Where can I turn for help?

❀ Taking care of myself is the most important thing I can do for my family. Where do I start?

"All sins tend to be addictive, and the terminal point of addiction is damnation."
—W. H. Auden, poet, 1907-1973

MAKING CHANGES

Wellness sometimes depends on our ability to make changes, but change is sooooo difficult! We know we should start exercising, eat better, make more time for our families, spend more time with our spouses. Change is so overwhelming and discouraging, especially if we've experienced brief bursts but no long-term success. Psychologists and psychiatrists tell us to find out what motivates our destructive behavior and make changes there first. For instance, if I don't exercise regularly, what motivates my poor behavior? Is my job too demanding? If so, perhaps the first change has to take place at work, not at the gym. Why do I continue to overeat? Am I comforting myself for a relationship I don't have? Perhaps change needs to occur on my social calendar before my diet.

1. Jot down a short list of five or six areas you would like to improve in your life.
2. Write down all the reasons why you have failed or are likely to fail to make each improvement.
3. Spend one month modifying or changing the things that block your success.
4. Spend the second month making the positive behavior a habit. Watch for the situations and circumstances that trigger behavior relapse. Change those situations or circumstances, and keep moving forward.
5. When you feel you have firmly established your new behavior, move on to the next item on your list. Spend the first month modifying or changing the things that might block your success before attempting to make the changes.

You are not going to experience any overnight changes. It might take you a year, or even two or three, to work through your list. But you're going to be one or two or three years older eventually. Wouldn't it be nice to be older and healthier?

Role Models

When our little baby girls are born and they are lying so tiny and pink in our arms, what do we wish for them? What kind of lives do we hope they will have? What sort of choices do we hope they will make? Many of their choices will be based on the choices we have made. It has come as a shock to the first generation of feminists to discover that many of their daughters aspire to be homemakers, not executives. What went wrong? After their mothers pushed open many doors and expanded the range of possibilities, why would young women today turn their backs on corporate opportunities and choose to stay at home?

Many young women are bitterly critical of their high-powered, executive mothers. Growing up as the daughters of successful women, they felt second-best, neglected, and abandoned. Their dreams are to become full-time homemakers and mothers. Their ambitions are to learn to cook, to make a home, and to spend time with their babies. Ironic, isn't it? They will learn, as their mothers did, that life is full of choices, not all of them easy, not all of them turning out the way we planned. Rather than modeling one choice versus another, wouldn't it be wonderful if we could model balance for our daughters?

THOUGHT TO PONDER

❀ How can I encourage my daughters to make wise and responsible choices even if their dreams are very different from mine?

"If you bungle raising your children, I don't think whatever else you do well matters very much."—Jacqueline Kennedy Onassis

RAISE YOUR CHILDREN WELL

I do not believe that rearing children well means the exclusion of all other activities and responsibilities, but I do believe rearing children well requires time and priority. Children are an all-consuming responsibility for a few years, and it may seem that life will always be so intense. But children grow up, and soon whatever we have left undone, unsaid, and untaught will remain so. Our job as a parent will be finished whether we think they, or we, are ready. If you have children at home, consider the following:

❀ Does each of my children have my undivided attention at least once every day?
❀ Do I start and end each day by letting my children know how much I love them?
❀ Do I know who my children's friends are, what their interests are, whom they admire?
❀ Have I established a tradition with each of my children that we can call ours?
❀ Am I home evenings and weekends even if they're not?
❀ Am I accessible to my children at any time?
❀ Am I comfortable talking to my children about God?
❀ Am I comfortable listening to my children talk about their beliefs?
❀ Am I willing to make hard choices on their behalf, if necessary?

Thinking Big

If you've ever attended a corporate motivational seminar, you have undoubtedly been encouraged, challenged, even bullied into thinking "big." "Big" means bigger sales, bigger departments, bigger profits, bigger commissions. Is bigger necessarily better? After the fallout from the crash of some of the world's largest companies, you would think the answer is only a qualified Maybe. But I bet that's not what your corporate trainer tells you. If you're in marketing or sales, you might even have a "Think Big" sign tacked to your bulletin board alongside pictures of cars, yachts, or exotic vacations. "Visualize success, and it will become a reality," promises the motivational guru.

Biblical teaching validates that technique. "By beholding we will become changed." We're just not thinking big enough. I once heard a Christian artist observe, "This life is like the opening act. It lasts about fifteen minutes, and it's not that great. Christians have tickets to the featured performance." If all we're aspiring to is the opening act, we're not thinking big enough.

THOUGHTS TO PONDER

❀ Materialism is seductive. How has it impacted my life?

❀ When is the last time I considered and challenged my idea of success?

"Don't confuse fame with success. Madonna is one; Helen Keller is the other."
—Erma Bombeck

FINDING YOUR WINGS

I don't know what God has in mind for you, but I bet it's much bigger than your dreams. We dream about things we think we can do. God plans for us to do things we were created to do. Often God allows us to live small, constrained lives, but I don't believe He plans for us to. Perhaps you are one of the lucky ones who feel God's power working miraculous things in your life. Perhaps you haven't found your place yet, and you're struggling. In teaching creativity classes, I have my students let  go of their preconceived ideas of who they are and what they are capable of and encourage them to dream. Often they find that very little is standing between them and what their heart has been secretly yearning for. I call it "finding your wings." Try the following exercise:

❀ Take out a sheet of paper, and as quickly as you can write, jot down all the careers you would like to try if you could start all over. Don't even consider the feasibility aspect at this point. You can write down "brain surgeon" AND "prima ballerina." Try to keep the pen on the paper and write as fast as you can. Try to fill up the entire page in less than five minutes.

❀ Take out a second sheet of paper. If time and money were no object, what things would you like to do or learn how to do? Again write as fast as you can. Try to fill up the entire page in less than five minutes.

❀ Now review your two pages. Circle the things that appeal to you most. What do you see? Do you see patterns, similarities, possibilities? Do they validate what you are doing now, or do they lead you to make some changes? Are there things you would like to do or be that would be feasible for you right now? Why not? Start small or start large—but start with something. God has built your interests into you. Trust your heart. Invite Him to lead. It will be safe to follow.

Wives and Warriors

God has called women to do the most extraordinary things. Deborah was chosen to lead an army; Esther was called to enter a beauty contest; Rahab was called to spy for the enemy; Ruth was asked to flirt with the landlord. It all worked out. God knew exactly what He was doing. Deborah led her troops to victory and saved God's people from annihilation. Esther became queen at a crucial moment and prevented a massacre of the Jewish people. Rahab harbored the Israelite spies, and she and her family survived the destruction of Jericho. Ruth agreed to follow her mother-in-law's quaint courting customs and became the great-grandmother of King David, an ancestor of the Messiah.

Do you think any of those women ever wondered whether they weren't crazy for following their hearts? I'm guessing that they second-guessed themselves a lot. I know I would. What am I doing in this harem? How did I ever let Mordicai talk me into this? I'm not that pretty. The king will never notice me. I'm going to spend the rest of my days attending to a bossy queen half my age and dying alone and childless. That's what would have been running through my mind. But Esther survived her doubts and saved a nation. It's not so much what it is that God calls us to do, it's the courage to do the right thing when the right thing becomes obvious. Deborah understood without a question that the Israelites needed someone to rally and lead them. Rahab believed with all her heart that the God of the Israelites was the one true God. Esther didn't flinch when thousands of lives hung in the balance. Ruth had grown to love her mother-in-law and was willing to trust her fully. Wives and warriors, beauty queens and spies, it doesn't matter whether we think we're important or not. If we have the courage to act with integrity, you and I can become instruments of God. Who's to say whose task is important or not?

THOUGHTS TO PONDER
- Do I live my life with integrity? Do I take pride in what I do?
- Can I trust God to lead me where I need to go?

"The talent of success is nothing more than doing what you can do well, and doing well whatever you do."—Henry Wadsworth Longfellow

IN HIS SERVICE

God has blessed women in this country with a profusion of choices. We can choose to be homemakers or entrepreneurs. We can develop personally, professionally, and creatively through an abundance of opportunities. Church is one place where we can give back some of what we have been blessed with. Church is a place to perform for His service. It doesn't matter whether we are leading a study group or cleaning the restrooms, we can perform it humbly for our Lord. There is no task so menial that it cannot be blessed by doing it to the glory of God. There is no task so difficult that it cannot be blessed by the outpouring of His Spirit. I try to remember this when I am cleaning up after a potluck as well as when I am asked to address the congregation. I am His handmaiden. He gets to choose where He will use me. To God be the glory! May my hands never become too fine or my heart too proud to perform humble service in the house of the Lord.

The Home Fires

When it comes to keeping the home fires burning, it doesn't matter whether we are CEOs of international corporations or stay-at-home moms. It is important to us. We crave a comfort zone where we can be safe and content and surrounded by the ones we love. As women, we are strongly motivated to provide that kind of space for our families. We expend a lot of energy "nesting." Whether it's a sleek urban loft or an old farmhouse, we desire to fill our homes with beautiful and meaningful things. So why is it that our homes so often feel like a battle zone, not a comfort zone? Perhaps it's because after all our time and trouble constructing a warm and inviting environment, the love of our life leaves his socks in the middle of the floor, and our adored children litter the house from one end to the other with papers, magazines, toys, and shoes. Our kids, who are the only ones who can program the VCR, are apparently technically challenged by changing a toilet-paper roll. It is easier to implement a coast-to-coast multimedia marketing campaign than it is to marshal the troops necessary to unload the dishwasher, fold the towels, or take out the garbage. At least that's the way it feels sometimes. If you think a solution comes later in the paragraph, I'm sorry, but you'll be disappointed. I believe every member of the family should be responsible for at least some of the chores, but I don't know how to live like Martha Stewart without an army of Martha's assistants. So amid the general clutter, we nag and cajole and sometimes threaten—but most often wind up picking up after the ones we love. I've got one more item for your to-do list. At least once before they go to bed tonight, tell everybody in your home how glad you are to be sharing a home and a life with them.

THOUGHTS TO PONDER

❀ If housework is a major issue in my home, what is one practical solution I can implement next week?

❀ Do I sometimes need to remind myself that the most beautiful thing about my home is the people who live in it?

CAMPFIRE DINNER
CAMPFIRE COOKING

The end of summer is a great time for one last family camping trip. These three campfire recipes are for foods that can be buried in the hot coals of an extinguished campfire and excavated three to four hours later for a warm, delicious meal. Preparation time: 20-25 minutes. Baking time: 35-45 minutes. Serves 6.

Pantry Items
Salt and pepper (to taste)
Heavy-duty aluminum foil
Brown sugar (1 cup)
Cinnamon powder (to sprinkle on baked apples)

Fresh Items
Baking potatoes (6 large)
Sweet onions (6)
Apples (6 large)
Corn on the cob (6 ears still in husks)
Butter or margarine (4 cubes)

DIRECTIONS
Make a campfire in an iron fire ring and let it burn completely down. Meanwhile, scrub potatoes and slice into 1-inch disks. Keep disks together in shape of potato. Peal and slice sweet onions into 1/2-inch rings (also keep together). On a square of aluminum foil, reassemble one potato and one onion by putting together 1 slice of potato, 1 pat of butter, 1 slice of onion, salt and pepper to taste. Repeat until potato is reassembled. Wrap tightly in foil. Core apple, pierce skin with fork. Add 1 pat of butter and 1 tablespoon brown sugar. Replace stem end (but not full core). Wrap tightly in foil. Wrap corn in foil. With aid of shovel, bury potatoes, apples, and corn deep in hot coals. Place hot coals on top of food. Cover with sand or earth to prevent any hot coals from starting a fire. Take a hike. Return a half hour later. Uncover food with shovel. Caution, Hot! Melted butter can run and burn. Use oven mitts to pick up. Sprinkle with cinnamon, if desired. Enjoy!

Destiny

Do you believe in destiny, or do you believe that things just happen to you? An ability to comprehend and accept your destiny must be a wonderful feeling. I don't think most women experience that kind of assurance and certainty. If you're like me, you suffer from a lot of uncertainty. Life is full of so many choices. I would personally be much happier if God would just FAX His agenda down so I could get on with life. Instead, my life has been full of stops and starts, good choices and bad. I never intended to make bad choices. In fact, some of the worst choices I've made have been choices I've labored over in prayer for a long time. Perhaps I should have labored longer. I've tried to follow God's will, but I have to admit I've gotten into some awful scrapes and endured some serious disappointments. Did God not hear my pleas for guidance, was I just not a good listener, or did I not work hard enough to make the plan work? I don't know. But I have discovered that no matter what happens, God is not far away. He rescues me in ways I could never have imagined. He comforts me with the most unexpected tenderness. In the midst of my shame, He opens my eyes and allows me a glimpse of His glory. He takes the grimy strands of my unraveling dreams and weaves me a coat of many colors. If my destiny is to experience the many ways God can love and care for a mere sinner woman in spite of her sinful self, I think I'm good with that. I guess I'm just destined to experience God's glory all the days of my life.

THOUGHTS TO PONDER

❀ Have I been able to see God's love and care running through my life?

❀ Does trusting in God keep me from making bad decisions?

"Grace is but glory begun, and glory is but grace perfected."
—*Jonathan Edwards, American theologian, 1703-1758*

FESTIVAL OF TENTS
CAMPING ACTIVITY

Ages: 5 to Adult
Materials Needed:
>   Tent
>   Sleeping bags
>   Camping equipment

Toward the end of summer, ancient Israel gathered in Jerusalem for a week of family camping to commemorate God's care over them in the wilderness after they left Egypt. The Israelites of old would construct temporary shelters out of palm branches and/or tents and camp out, retell stories of God's deliverance, and sing together. Sounds like fun, doesn't it? The Bible refers to this holiday as the Feast of Tabernacles or the Festival of Tents. Many Jews today still celebrate this holiday and construct temporary structures in their yards or at campsites. The end of summer is a great time to take one last family camping trip. On this camping trip, read about the Exodus deliverance together. Talk about how God is going to come and take us all home to the New Jerusalem soon. Discus how our lives on this earth are only temporary until Jesus takes us home. Illustrating God's love and care while having a great time together is what celebration is all about!

The Eye of the Storm

When I was a very small girl, a hurricane passed over the island where we lived. We were tucked safely inside the thick stone walls of our home with the wooden shutters latched and barred. Outside, the storm raged all night and most of the day. In mid-afternoon the winds stopped completely, not a breeze, not even a whisper. The radio warned that the storm was not over. The eye of the hurricane was passing directly over us. Within the hour the backside of the storm would hit, and the winds would slam against the island from the opposite direction. On an impulse, my father ordered us into our raincoats and boots and loaded us into the station wagon. He drove the short distance to the lighthouse, and we piled out on to the deserted promenade. From our vantage point above the island, we could see the destruction the storm had wreaked; downed trees and debris covered the once gardenlike landscape. Out on the horizon we could see the backside of the storm advancing like a black wall. It was impossible to tell where the sea and sky met. As the storm approached, the winds grew stronger, and the surf slammed against the rocks below, spraying foam and water high above onto the walkway. We hung on to the railing, wildly exhilarated, as the wind and sea whipped at our faces. It was only for a few minutes. My parents quickly piled us back into the car, and we sped back to our little cottage as leaves and branches blew past the window. By the time the full force of the storm hit, we were safely inside our home with the shutters barred.

As mothers in the twenty-first century, it sometimes feels as if we live our lives in the eye of the storm. We want to protect our families from the destructive forces of the world. We want to keep our children safe from the frightening choices that surround them. Wouldn't be wonderful if we could pull the shutters and bar the door? Of course, we can't. We can only point our children to safety; we can introduce them early and often to the One who can keep them safe, no matter how hard the winds blow.

THOUGHTS TO PONDER
❀ Do I take time to talk to my children about practical Christianity?
❀ Do my children see my relationship with God in my life?

> *"The wise man in the storm prays to God, not for safety from danger, but for deliverance from fear."—Ralph Waldo Emerson*

GARDEN GIFTS

Sharing from our garden is one of the most heartfelt expressions of friendship we can bestow. Whether we have cultivated a vegetable or a flower garden, the fruits of our labor are deeply appreciated gifts, even if they come in a paper sack or a canning jar. But when we take the time to present them in a special way, the recipient feels special indeed. A few ideas:

Cut Flowers. Vases can be picked up inexpensively at flea markets and discount stores. Even a plain vase looks beautiful with fresh flowers and a bow. Leave an arrangement on a neighbor's doorstep or, better yet, make a delivery to some lucky person's office. It will make their day!

Garden Vegetables. If your garden is overflowing with more abundance than your family can consume, you will want to share your bounty. Instead of a paper sack, consider a basket or pretty pail in which to present your garden gifts. Include a favorite recipe or two featuring your produce. For an extra-special gift, add a box of pasta or a bottle of your favorite salad dressing.

Fruit. We all love to receive homegrown fruit. The special ways we can present homegrown berries and fruit is endless: fresh fruit in a basket with a bow, freezer bags of fruit in an inexpensive picnic cooler, canned fruit in jars decorated with fabric bows or lid covers, homemade fruit preserves and jellies, even homemade applesauce and pies.

God is good! What a joy it is to share the bounties of His abundance.

Letting Go

When do you let go? When is a relationship, a job, a dream so badly battered that you have to let it slip away before it pulls you under? When does hanging on become counter-productive? Winston Churchill once addressed a group of graduates with the simple instructions, "Never, never, never, never, give up!" And then he sat down. As useful as that advice may have been for England, I have not found it very practical in everyday life. The jobs, relationships, and dreams that I have clung to as if my life depended on them have nearly pulled me under.

As women, we often assume it is our responsibility to make things work for our children, our families, our spouses, and our employers while it becomes increasingly obvious that nothing is working for us. Why do we put ourselves in such unhealthful situations? We must be getting something out of it, or we would have bailed out of the situation long before. Perhaps sacrificing our lives to do our so-called duty makes us feel important and needed, but it's a short-term gain. We can never make up for the lack in someone else's life, no matter how much we care about them. Enablers eventually wind up crippling the ones they are trying to help. The crippled one is never appreciative, only crippled. Sometimes the best we can do is to stop trying to fix shattered dreams and start living the life we have been given. Sometimes the best we can do is to let go.

THOUGHTS TO PONDER
- ❀ Have I ever stayed in a bad job or poor relationship because I was afraid to let go?
- ❀ Is there someone in my life I am "helping" too much? Can I move into a more appropriate relationship, or do I need to let go?

"Perseverance is failing 19 times and succeeding the 20th."
—Julie Andrews

TOO PROUD TO FAIL

Are you too proud to fail? If you are, you are undoubtedly stuck in some very dysfunctional situations. It would be great if everything in life worked out, but it doesn't, and in a lifetime we are bound to embark on some ventures that won't turn out as we anticipated. If we can admit our failures, we can acquire valuable lessons and move forward. Otherwise, we are just doomed to repeat our mistakes time and time again.

Perhaps your fear of failure keeps you from trying. Better to stay stuck in a miserable situation than to try something new. This is not a very good plan either. Following are some myths about failure that keep us stuck and ineffective. The sooner we debunk them, the sooner we can move into more fulfilling and productive lives:

Myth 1. Failure indicates lack of character.
Myth 2. Failure indicates a poor relationship with God.
Myth 3. Failure happens only to bad people.

Consider that one of our greatest presidents failed in business twice, lost eight elections out of ten, and suffered a nervous breakdown before being elected to the presidency of the United States. Who was this failure? Abraham Lincoln. Thank God he wasn't too proud to fail! Failure is not sin, but being too proud to admit failure might be.

Hanging On

When the best you can do is to let go, what do you hang on to? Failure is an event we are usually not prepared to deal with. Divorce, loss, layoffs can be hugely disorienting. Here is my personal "Top Ten List of Things to Hang on to When Letting Go."

#10—Hang on to your dignity. Failure may feel awful, but it is only something that has happened to you. It is not who you are. Some of the most successful people in history have experienced deep personal failures. You are in good company.

#9—Hang on to your sanity. Failure is an enormous blow. Expect to feel sad, angry, hurt, and devastated in quick succession. Give yourself permission to experience your emotions and understand that they are normal. Seeking out a professional counselor can help you navigate the turbulence.

#8—Hang on to your health. Your system has sustained an awful shock. Now is not the time to start bingeing on anything. Take care of yourself, eat well, continue to exercise, go to bed on time.

#7—Hang on to your friends. Even if you just feel like crawling into a hole, let your friends support and comfort you. They are the network that will help you rebuild your life.

#6—Hang on to your sense of humor. Nothing that we can laugh at can conquer us. Even black humor is cathartic. There is a fine line between tragedy and comedy. Cross it!

#5—Hang on to your family. Whatever group constitutes a family for you, those whom you have a history with, who knew you before when . . . hang on to them for perspective.

#4—Hang on to your integrity. Failure does not make you a bad person. Don't act like one, and don't feel like one.

#3—Hang on to your judgment. It is easy to feel desperate following a failure. Don't jump into anything. Give yourself some time to sort through your options.

#2—Hang on to your children. Protect them as much as possible. They should not have to experience disturbing adult emotions. Take time to love and reassure them; they will sense all is not well with you. Let them see you happy too.

#1—Hang on to your God. He will not only sustain you through the darkest hours, but He also has a miraculous way of turning your failures into triumphs for His glory. Give Him time.

"Failure after long perseverance is much grander than never to have a striving good enough to be called a failure."—George Eliot, British novelist, 1819-1880

FIVE STAGES OF RECOVERY

Living through a major life failure such as a divorce, loss of a job, or a financial failure is similar in many respects to surviving a death. Except that the loss involved is our own loss of identity. It is helpful to understand that the emotional stages are a part of the healing process and that we will survive.

1. Shock
2. Denial
3. Anger
4. Grief
5. Acceptance

It's not really possible to skip any of the steps. If we try to, the process just takes longer. Each step can take a few weeks to some months. Each step is important in helping us process our loss and learn from the experience. At each step I have found my heavenly Father gently holding my hand and providing comfort in the most unexpected ways. Failure doesn't just have to be failure; with God's miraculous grace, it can be a new beginning.

From Whence Cometh My Help

It is so easy to fool ourselves into believing that help comes from personal political clout, a bank account, or a steady job. But sooner or later in every life, we face the fact that those things can't help when it really counts. No amount of money can keep a loved one from dying. All the personal clout in the world can't reverse declining health. There is nothing a good job can do to prevent a child from making self-destructive choices. When we face loss, illness, or the pain of watching the ones we love suffer, we are helpless. It doesn't matter how rich or powerful or important we are. Life is the great equalizer. Princes and paupers, sinners and saints—we are all subject to the frailty of life on a sinful planet. Even if we put our trust in God, we are still not exempt from loss and pain.

The Bible indicates that as Christians we may experience even more suffering and loss. So is there no help? God does not promise to protect us from death and suffering. They are a part of living in an evil world. Our only hope is an escape, not a cure. As smart as human beings are, we are incapable of making this world exempt from death and pain. As powerful as God is, He cannot make sin right. Sin is always destructive, always disruptive. Our help comes from a God who will one day wipe away all tears and create a world made new. We have a peace that comes from understanding that our pain is the pain of new birth, not of death. Our help comes from a God who faithfully finds a way to reach out and comfort us in even our darkest hours. This world is not our home. Through the grace of God, someday soon our hearts will find a home.

THOUGHTS TO PONDER

❀ How do I teach my children to trust God and at the same time help them realize that even Christians suffer?

❀ Do I sometimes assume that because I am a Christian, God will protect me from all the bad things?

"Out of suffering have emerged the strongest souls; the most massive characters are seared with scars."—Edwin H. Chapin, 1814-1880

PAIN AND BEAUTY

Artists have often found that their most painful experiences have given birth to their greatest achievements. Are there dark moments in your life that seem to haunt you? Now is an excellent time to submit your sorrows to your creative process. Try the following creativity exercise. You don't need to be an artist. You will find this experience wonderfully cathartic.

1. Before you begin, you must set aside at least forty-five minutes of isolated, uninterrupted time.
2. Set a large sheet of paper in front of you and several sharpened pencils.
3. Close your eyes and recall your most painful experience in as much detail as possible. What did it feel like, smell like, sound like? When you are ready, pick up your pencil.
4. Start to write or draw. Do not take your pencil off the paper for forty-five minutes. Keep your pencil moving. If you are drawing, try drawing only shapes and lines, not real objects. If you are writing, write free-flowing thoughts, words, and associations, not paragraphs and stories. Cover the entire page. Stay focused on your emotions. Use your pencil to freely express your feelings. If the point breaks, that's OK. Pick up another one. If you run out of space, turn the paper over or just draw/write on top. Stop after forty-five minutes.

Put your paper away for a few days, and then come back to it. You will be amazed at what you see. In my art classes, I have found that this exercise never fails to yield fertile seeds for new creative projects.

Winds of Change

The role of women in our society has changed. We have more opportunities, more challenges, more responsibilities. Old stereotypes have crumbled and disintegrated. Women are no longer expected to be only the secretary to the boss, the nurse to the doctor, the power behind the throne. We are executives, doctors, and leaders, as well as secretaries, nurses, and wives. The winds of change have replaced old prejudices and boundaries with more choices. Choices can be very threatening. Some women yearn for the days when their lives were more clearly defined. A time when expectations were more concrete. Choices require deliberate thought and examination. It is much easier to allow the expectations of our family and community to map out a course for us. But that has never been the way of Christians.

When we chose Christ, we chose to become the woman God has created us to be. He did not consult society's expectations when He knit us in the womb, when He imbued us with talents, when He called us into service. We have a role to play on this earth and throughout eternity. Although our roles as Christian women may be diverse, our purpose is the same. We are here to glorify God, and by allowing our lives to be a conduit for His purpose, we experience great joy. It is the most incredibly satisfying experience to do the thing that we were created to do, to do it well, and to do it with all our might to the glory of God. We should accept no criticism and make no excuses for who we are. We must extend the same acceptance and affirmation to our sisters as well and allow no one to criticize their calling either, be it homemaker or president. We have many talents, but we are of the same body, and Christ alone is our head. Only He has the authority to appoint and direct how we will be used. As Christian women, we are happily at His service, whatever our calling may be.

THOUGHTS TO PONDER

❀ Am I doing what God has appointed me to do, or do I feel a persistent desire to reexamine my choices?

❀ Am I ever subject to criticism for following the path I believe God had laid out for me?

"To serve is beautiful, but only if it is done with joy and a whole heart and a free mind."
—*Pearl S. Buck*

GOD'S COMMUNITY SERVICE

Dale Twomley was president of Worthington Foods, Inc., for a number of years. He is one of the busiest men I've known, and I learned a valuable lesson watching him. It's a hard lesson. It's not an easy one to put in practice. There have been times I've wished his example didn't haunt and dog me. During the four years we attended the same church, I noticed that Mr. Twomley was always one of the last ones to leave after an event. He could be found mopping up the floor, picking up the chairs, wiping down the counters, taking out the trash. It wasn't once in a while; it wasn't just when it was his group putting on the event. It was every time. I couldn't help acknowledging the obvious. If the president of a large multimillion-dollar corporation could find the time to perform the most humble service on behalf of his local church and school, I really didn't have a good excuse not to. I can't tell you how many times I've walked back into a church kitchen or school gym because of Mr. Twomley's example. I've heard it said that charity begins at home. Mr. Twomley practiced that principle. Picking up chairs, mopping the floor, washing the punch bowls, when performed in God's service, such tasks are privileges every Christian should cherish.

Choices

God gives (wo)man freedom of choice. In fact, God is insistent on our divine right to choose. A god who destroys those who do not choose him is not offering a choice. Nor is a god who programs us to choose only him. On the other hand, an entity that defies God and desires to control and manipulate our choices is not providing us with free exercise of the will either. Our choices were abdicated when Eve chose to separate herself from God. Up until that point, her freedom of choice was intact. But once she chose, she could not undo her choice. It took a God to do that—and at what a cost! As Eve's daughters, we are born flawed and imperfect.

Through the death of Christ, our freedom of choice is restored. We are free again, like Eve, to choose good or to choose evil. What an awesome thought that a deity would die to preserve our right to choose, even if it meant the right to choose evil over good. Existence without choice is simply not acceptable to God. How very respectful we must be of one another's choices. Our right to choose has been purchased by divine blood. Today we have a choice. Today we can choose for our will to be done or for His will to be done. Either way, God will respect our choice. As Christians, shouldn't we do the same?

THOUGHT TO PONDER

❀ When a friend or coworker makes a choice that I do not approve of, is it better for me to speak out against her choice or for me to respect the choice?

CURRY RICE SALAD
SEASONAL PRODUCE

This is a pretty end-of-summer salad full of fruits and vegetables. Boil rice: 20 minutes. Preparation Time: 20 minutes. Refrigerate: overnight. Serves 8–10.

Pantry Items
Uncooked rice (2 cups)
Toasted almonds (1/2 cup, chopped)
Golden raisins (1/2 cup)
Dried cranberries (1/2 cup)
Cumin (1 Tbsp.)
Chicken-style seasoning (1 Tbsp.)
Salt and pepper (to taste)
Mayonnaise (1 cup)

Fresh Items
Celery (2 stalks)
Green onions (1 cup, chopped)
Apple (1)
Firm tofu (1 block)

DIRECTIONS
Bring 4 cups of water to boil. Mix in uncooked rice, bring to boil, reduce heat to low, cover and cook until water is absorbed. Meanwhile, place tofu in colander to drain. (Press gently to remove as much excess liquid as possible.) Dice celery, green onions, and apple. Mix together in large bowl with almonds, raisins, and cranberries. Cut drained tofu into 1/2-inch cubes. Add cooled rice, cumin, chicken-style seasoning, salt, pepper, and mayonnaise to mixture in bowl and mix well. Add tofu last. Fold in gently. Cover and refrigerate for 4 hours or overnight. Mix gently before serving.

SUBSTITUTION: You may substitute a can of drained diced soy chicken in place of tofu.

A Place at the Table

Well we've finally earned our right to a place at the table. Even though only a handful of women hold the coveted executive chairs of our nation's largest public corporations, a few do, and there is no turning back. After years of being passed over for promotions, receiving backhanded compliments on our dresses, enduring crude jokes about "that time of month," and waiting for golf invitations that were never extended, we are finally seeing doors of the good ole' boys club swing open. Aren't we? I sure hope so. Bigotry is ugly in any form.

Recently, I've seen young men and women working side by side with seemingly no concern about gender roles from either sex. Young women are open about their intentions to take time off to have a family, and it doesn't seem to cost their career advancement the way it did in earlier generations. I wish these young people well. The future is theirs. I hope they hold on to their ideals and stand firm for their principles. I hope getting ahead no longer means sacrificing time with children or family for either parent. I hope the excesses of the late twentieth century have taught us that single-minded focus on a career is not a productive or satisfying life. I hope we've learned a few painful lessons from our obsession with "everything all the time." I have my doubts, but I also have my hopes. Now that both men and women have a seat at the table, I wonder, what will we accomplish together? I have my doubts, but I also have my hopes.

THOUGHTS TO PONDER

❀ A 2002 survey reported that 65 percent of women still prefer male supervisors. Are we really still that jealous of one another?

❀ What can I do to challenge bigotry in my office or workplace?

"If when a businessman speaks of minority employment, or air pollution, or poverty, he speaks in the language of a certified public accountant analyzing a corporate balance sheet, who is to know that he understands the human problems behind the statistical ones? If the businessman would stop talking like a computer printout or a page from the corporate annual report, other people would stop thinking he had a cash register for a heart. It is as simple as that—but that isn't simple."—Louis B. Lundborg

TOWER OF BABEL
INSIDE OR OUTSIDE ACTIVITY

Ages: 3 to Adult
Materials Needed:
Lightweight cardboard boxes
Empty pasta boxes
Empty cereal boxes
Shoeboxes
Small cardboard boxes
Office supply boxes (such as envelope and stationery boxes)
Craft paper or wrapping paper (optional)

This is a fun game that the entire family can play. The object of the game is to try to build the tallest tower out of the boxes before it topples over. Collect lightweight cardboard boxes for a few weeks. Try to collect as many different box sizes as possible. Cover with craft paper or wrapping paper if desired. You can use paper grocery bags to cover the boxes, and the entire project can go into the recycling bin when you're finished playing. Small children enjoy knocking the tower down as much as building it. Older kids enjoy the challenge of constructing the tallest structure. Play the game outside for an additional challenge. The wind will add an extra element to the balancing act.

If you enjoyed this book, you'll enjoy these as well:

GARDENS OF THE SOUL

Debbonnaire Kovacs. The care and nurture of your inner devotional life is the topic of this unique "gardening" guide. Drawing from her own background as a gardener, Debbonnaire uses a spiritual gardening allegory and her study of God's Word to teach us practical ways to cultivate a flourishing devotional life with God.

    0-8163-1872-7. Paperback.

    US$12.99, Can$20.99.

DEVOTIONAL RETREATS

Debbonnaire Kovacs. Draw closer to Jesus through devotional retreats—a method of using your five senses to study God's Word. Kovacs explains the purpose and joy of Christian meditation, and how it differs from the New Age counterfeit.

    0-8163-1837-9. Paperback.

    US$4.97, Can$7.97.

TIME FOR ALL THAT'S IMPORTANT

Tamyra Horst. Tired of being sick and tired? This book will show you how to stop living like a gerbil and start finding time for the things that really matter. Be who God made you to be, say No without guilt, define and stick to your priorities, and find the balance between "doing" and "being" in this intensely practical book.

    0-8163-1783-6. Paperback.

    US$4.97, Can$7.97.

Order from your ABC by calling **1-800-765-6955**, or get online and shop our virtual store at <www.AdventistBookCenter.com>.

- Read a chapter from your favorite book
- Order online
- Sign up for email notices on new products

Prices subject to change without notice.